MINUS 31 AND THE WIND BLOWING

MINUS 31 AND THE WIND BLOWING

9 REFLECTIONS ABOUT LIVING ON LAND

John Haines
Thomas LeDuc
Monroe Price
Walter Parker
Robert Durr
Margaret Murie
Joseph Meeker
Wm. Kloefkorn
Gary Snyder

ALASKA PACIFIC UNIVERSITY PRESS
1980

This is Alaskana Book No. 37
Published by Alaska Pacific University Press, Anchorage, AK 99504

This book is published under a grant of the Alaska Humanities Forum and the National Endowment of the Humanities

International Standard Book Number: 0-935094-01-6
Printed in the United States of America

FIRST EDITION

CONTENTS

INTRODUCTION
Gary H. Holthaus

I

PABLO NERUDA, the great poet and statesman of the southern hemisphere, said,

> Poetry is an action, ephemeral or solemn in which are joined as equal partners solitude and solidarity, emotion and action, the nearness of one's self, the nearness to mankind and to the secret manifestations of nature.

He went on to say

> No less strongly than this, I think, is sustained man and his shadow, man and his conduct, man and his poetry. These are sustained by an ever-wider sense of community, by an effort which will forever bring together the reality and the dream in us.

To bring together the reality and the dream in us; to consider carefully what it is that is important about our lives as individuals and our life together in Alaska, and to project both the reality and the dream onto the far larger screen of an uncertain future — that is the purpose of the papers which have been collected in this book.

II

Why do Alaskans talk so much about land and lifestyles? Because land is the crucial issue in the state; because a number of critical land use issues confront us now and in the immediate future, and because some of the land use decisions we have made in the last seven or eight years are beginning to have a very visible effect upon the towns and villages in which we live. They are having a less visible, but perhaps even more important effect upon our attitudes, our election outcomes, our personal freedom. So land is crucial for us all. It can bind us together or it can pull us apart. In it we may find some essential unity, or we may let it draw us into the destruction of racism and economic strife. The public policy decisions about land are too critical to leave entirely to the agency people, the "experts."

With all our differences of culture and lifestyle in this state, we are one people, and it is the land which unites us. We may destroy ourselves over it, but we are *of* the earth. Its essence is our own and the old creation stories have their own truth. We are made of the earth, and when we destroy the land's health, we destroy our own as well. In our saner moments we know that we are one with all mankind and with the earth, for we all live in a subsistence relationship to the land. All our economies, regardless of cash flows, credit or stocks, or other media for the exchange of values, are essentially subsistence economies based upon what the land has to offer by way of energy and raw material.

Although our underground resources are not as mobile as the caribou herd, nor renewable as fish, nor susceptible to domestication as plants, our pursuit of natural resources for energy and material for the subsistence of our culture is remarkably similar to that of the aboriginal hunter. The nomadic oil geologist and the peripatetic prospector are both part of a culture which is rooted directly in an ancient and inescapable tradition of dependence upon the land.

Among other things which the energy crisis reveals about our culture, our economy and our selves, is simply this — we are hunters still, and when the land no longer provides for our needs, we will starve. In the "old way," when the caribou failed to come, people went hungry. In our new way, when the energy sources begin to fade, General Motors puts 38,000 men out of work, and we experience the contemporary equivalent of hunger pangs.

III

So we must consider the land, meditate upon it, brood about it, for I suspect that there, more surely than any place else, lies the secret reason for our being, our purposes, our relationships to one another, to the Creator of us all, and to the mystery of who we are and what we might become.

It is in the land that we will discover from whence we came, our proper place in the present and our prospect for the future. These all lie buried in the tundra, the mountains and the seas, and in the ceaseless movement of the creatures, including man, who depend upon them for life.

To live upon this Alaskan land, and with one another, with as little damage as possible, reflecting thoughtfully about our choices and our opportunities to create and maintain a lifestyle we can continue to love — this is a task which requires us all, the scientist and the shaman, the business man and the artist, the humanist and the holy man.

In these papers you will find no solutions to specific policy questions. You will find a variety of attitudes toward the land, visions of its many different aspects, the insight of people who lived upon it thoughtfully, and who have been willing to share their perceptions and perspectives with us. Diverse as these papers are, they ask only that you think deeply and carefully about what it means to live upon this land now and in the future.

IN WILDERNESS

THREE DAYS
John Haines

I

SIX O'CLOCK on a January morning. I wake, look into the darkness overhead, and then to the half-lighted windows. I listen. No sound comes to me from the world outside. The wind is quiet.

I get out of bed, pulling the stiffness from my body. Jo is still sleeping under the big down robe, turned toward the wall. I go to the window with a flashlight and look out at the thermometer. It is minus 31, clear, and no moon. It will not be light for another three hours.

I put on a jacket and a pair of slippers, and go outside. The door creaks on its frosty hinges, the latch is cold to my hand. One of our dogs emerges from his house in the yard and shakes himself, rattling his chain.

The stars are bright, Orion gone down the west. The Dipper has turned, Arcturus above the hill. The sky and the snow give plenty of light, and I can easily see the outlines of the river channel below the house, and the dark crests of the hills around me. The air is sharp and clean, it will be a good day.

I gather up a few sticks of wood from the porch and go back indoors. Laying the wood on the floor beside the stove, I go to a table by the south window, find a match, and light the lamp. I turn the wick up slowly, letting the chimney warm.

Light gathers in the room, reflecting from the window glass and the white enamel of a washpan. I open the stove door and the damper in the pipe. With a long poker I reach into the big firebox and rake some of the hot coals forward. I lay kindling on them, dry slivers of spruce, and two or three dry sticks on top of these. I close the door and open the draft. Air sucks through the draft holes, and in no time the fire is burning, the wood crackling. I fill the big kettle with water from a bucket near at hand, and set it on the back of the stove. It will soon be singing.

By now Jo is awake and beginning to function. I sit on the edge of the bed, putting thoughts together. The lamp makes shadows in the small room; heat is beginning to flow from the stove.

Today I am going back to our cabin below Banner Dome, to look at my traps. I have not been out for over a week, and must surely have caught something by now. While Jo makes breakfast, I begin to dress. We talk a little; the mornings here are quiet, the days also.

I put on heavy wool trousers over my underwear, and two wool shirts. Over the wool trousers I sometimes wear another light cotton pair to break the wind or to keep off the snow. I put on socks — three pair of wool, and the felt oversock; two pair of insoles, and last the moosehide moccasins. I tie them at the top; they are a loose fit, soft and light on my feet. I made them six years ago from the hide of a big moose, and though worn by now, they are still the best I have.

I go out to the storehouse, find my big basket, and begin to pack. I will need my small axe, a few traps, and perhaps a few snares. That piece of dried moose paunch I have been saving — it is strong-smelling and will make good bait. What else? Something needed for the cabin — a candle, some kerosene in a bottle. I put it all together in the basket.

We eat our breakfast slowly, there is no hurry. Half-frozen blueberries with milk, oatmeal, bread, and plenty of coffee. We listen to the stove, to the kettle buzzing. How many winters have gone by like this? Each morning that begins in the same quiet way — the darkness, the fire, the lamp, the stirring within. We talk a little, what she will do when I am gone. Food will have to be cooked for the dogs, there is plenty of wood. I am not sure when I will return; in three days, maybe.

By 7:30 I am ready. I get my stuff together — into the basket now goes a light lunch, some bread for the cabin. I put on my old green army parka with its alpaca lining buttoned into it. It is heavily patched, and by now almost a homemade thing, the hood sewn large and trimmed with fur to shield my face from the wind. I take two wool caps, one for my head, and another in the basket in case I should need it. My big mittens also go into the pack; to start with, I will need only a pair of canvas gloves.

8

I say goodbye at the door, and walk up the hill. The dogs think that they may be going too, and the four of them begin to bark, waiting for the harness and tugging at their chains. But today I am going on foot; I want to take my time, to look around and set new traps. My dogs are too much in a hurry.

×

I begin the long climb through the birchwoods to the ridge. The trail goes steeply the first few hundred yards, but it soon takes an easier grade, turning north and away from the river. The woods are still dark, but there is light in the snow, and perhaps a brightening in the sky above the trees. Morning and evening come on slowly this time of year, a gradual twilight. I carry a light walking stick made of birch in one hand as I go along. It comes in handy, to knock snow off the brush, to test the ice when I cross a creek, or to kill an animal with when I find one alive in a trap.

It is a winter of light snowfall, with barely ten inches on the ground, and I do not need my snowshoes. The trail is packed hard underfoot, and is easy walking, but away in the woods the snow is still loose and powdery under a thin crust; in the dim light I see that it is littered with dry, curled leaves and small, winged seeds from the alders and birches.

The air is sharp on my face, and it pinches my nose, but I soon begin to feel warm from climbing. I open my parka and push the cap back on my head; I take off my gloves and put them into one of my pockets. It won't do to get overheated.

Behind me now I hear an occasional mournful howl from one of our dogs, sunken and distant in the timber. Otherwise, there is not a sound in the woods this morning, and no air moving in the trees. But now and then the quiet snap of something contracting or expanding in the frost. At other times I have walked this trail in deep snow and bright moonlight, when the birch shadows made another transparent forest on the snow. There were shadows within the shadows, and now and then something would seem to move there — rabbit or lynx, or only a shape in my mind.

Partway up the hill I come to a marten set. Earlier in the season I caught a marten here, close to home, but there is nothing in the trap this morning. In the grey light I see that nothing has come to it, and all the tracks in the snow around it are old.

Frost bristles on the trap, a dense white fur over the jaws, the pan and the trigger. I put my gloves back on, spring the trap and bang it a couple of times against the pole to knock the frost from it.

I have two ways of setting traps for marten — one on the snow, and the other on a pole above the snow. This is a pole set. To make it, I have cut down a young birch four feet above the snow, and drawn the trunk of the tree forward a couple of feet to rest in the vee of the stump. I split the end of it to take a piece of bait, and the trap is set back a short space on top of the pole and held in place with a piece of light wire or string. It is a good way in heavy snow; once caught, the marten will always be found hanging from the pole.

Satisfied that the trap is working properly, I reset it, tying the wire loosely in place again. I go on, walking at a steady pace as the trail levels and climbs, winding among the birches.

×

Within half an hour I come out of the trees and into the open on the long, cleared ridge that rises behind the homestead. Light is stronger here, and I can see the cold, blue height of Banner Dome to the north beyond a range of hills. I have a long ways to go.

I begin to cool off now that I am on top, so I wear my gloves and button the front of my parka. As I stride along in the lightly drifted snow, I savor once more the cold stillness of this winter morning — my breath blown in a long plume before me, and no sound but the soft crunch of my moccasins, and the grating of my stick in the snow.

This ridge like a true watershed divides what I like to think of as my country; for in a way I own it, having come by it honestly, and nearly its oldest resident now. To the south of me, all the way down to the river, it is mostly dry hillside with birch and aspen. To the north, falling away into Redmond and Banner Creeks, it is spruce country, mossy and wet. Years ago, when I first lived here, this ridge was heavily wooded; the trail wound through the timber, companionable and familiar, with small clearings and berry patches. Then, eight years ago, came a pipeline crew clearing the

10

ridges and hillsides into Fairbanks. And later they built a powerline to run beside it, from Fairbanks to Delta. The cleared way is overgrown with grass, with alders and raspberries, and the pipe is buried in the ground; but the ridge is windy now, and the trail drifts badly in heavy snow. Because of this, few fur animals come here, and I have no traps on this ridge.

I see some much-trampled snow at the edge of the timber, and turn aside to look. Moose have been feeding here at night, and the tops of many of the smaller trees are pulled down, broken and bitten. I find a couple of hard-packed beds in the snow, and piles of black, frozen droppings. The moose must be close by, but they are out of sight, bedded down in the timber. I stand very still and listen, but hear nothing.

I cover a good mile of steady walking as the light grows and the snow brightens; the trail visible now some distance ahead of me where it follows the open ridge, paced by the power poles, dipping and curving with the slope of the hills. And then near the top of the last rise of hill the trail swings sharply north, and I go down into the woods again. The country changes swiftly, becomes dense and shaggy, the scrubby black spruce dominant, with alder and a few scattered birches. The trail is narrow, rutted and uneven to walk. There is more snow here on a north slope, and I soon see marten sign, their characteristic tracks crossing my trail at intervals.

I have gone only a short distance when I find a marten dead in a trap, it is frozen, hanging head down at the end of the trap chain — a female, small, and with dull orange splashes over its neck and shoulders, a grizzled mask on its frost-pinched face. I release it from the trap and put the hard, stiff body in my pack. I cut a fresh piece of bait and reset the trap — where one marten has been caught, the chances are good for another.

Encouraged by my luck, in good spirits I go on, following the trail through the woods, turning and climbing, past windfalls and old, rotted firestumps under the snow. A small covy of spruce hens startles me, flying up from the snow into the trees with a sudden flurry of wings. I hear an alarmed clucking, and see one of the big black and grey birds perched on a spruce bough, sitting very still but watching me with one bright eye.

On a point of hill where a stand of birches form an open grove, I stop for a short time to rest and reset a trap. The sun is up now, just clearing the hills to the south. There is light in the trees, a gold light laid on the blue and white of the snow, and luminous shadows. Frost-crystals glitter in the still air wherever a shaft of sunlight pierces the forest.

This hill is open to the north, and I can see, closer now, the rounded summit of Banner Dome, rose and gold in the low sunlight. The Salchaket hills rising beyond it stand out clearly in the late morning sunlight. I can just see part of the shoulder of hill that rises above the cabin I am going to, six miles yet by this trail. The valleys of Redmond and Glacier Creeks lie below me, still in a deep, cold shadow. The sun will not reach there for another month. I keep a cache on this hill, a 50 gallon oil drum with a tight lid bolted to it. I brought it here on the sled a couple of years ago, on the last snow of the season. It stands upright between two birches, with its rusty grey paint a little out of place here in the woods, but to me familiar. Inside it I keep a few traps, a spare axe, and some cans of emergency rations in case I should need them. Whatever I leave there stays dry and is safe from bears.

I stand with my pack off for a moment, leaning on my stick. A little wind from somewhere stirs in the birches overhead. I have sometimes thought of building a small camp here, a shelter under these trees. There are places we are attracted to more than others, though I do not always know why. Here, it is the few strong birches, the airy openness of the woods, the view, and the blueberry shrubs under the trees where in good years we have come to pick them. If I were to begin again in some more distant part of the country, to build a home, this is one place I would consider. Perhaps because I know it so well, it is already part of what I think of as home.

I take up my pack and stick, ready to go on. I have put on my mittens, finally; my gloves have gotten damp and become icy and stiff on my hands. From here the trail descends the long north slope into Redmond, a wandering, downhill track through stubby open spruce and over much boggy ground, the longest hill I have to walk. As soon as I start down I am out of the sunlight and into shadow again. It feels at once colder, with a chill blue light in the snowy hummocks.

It is six years now since I cut this part of the trail, and it is worn deep in the moss from our summer walking. So little snow this winter, it makes hard foot and sled travel over the humps and holes. So I walk, going from one side of the trail to the other, springing from hummock to hummock, and balancing myself with my stick. I go at a good pace, anxious to cover the remaining ground before the day is over.

×

I am halfway down the hill when I find another marten in a trap set on the snow under a spruce. The marten is still alive, tugging at the end of the trap chain, angry and snarling. For a moment I stand and look at the animal. No larger than a housecat, but supple and snaky in body, it lunges at me as if it would bite me.

I take off my pack and approach the marten with my stick. I hit it a sharp blow across its nose, and it falls twitching in the snow. I quickly turn it on its back, lay my stick across its throat and hold it there with one foot, while I place my other foot on its narrow chest. I can feel the small heart beating through the sole of my moccasin.

As I stand bending over it, the marten partly revives and attempts to free itself, kicking and squirming. But in a short time its heart stops and the slim body relaxes. I remove my foot and the stick, open the trap jaws, and lay the marten out in the snow. It is a large, dark male with thick fur.

It is better to find them dead and frozen, I do not like to kill them this way. Mostly they do not live long when caught in a trap in cold weather; another few hours, and this one too would have frozen.

I reset the trap at the bottom of the tree, placing it on two small dry sticks. I arrange the toggle stick so that the marten will have to step over it and into the trap. I cut a fresh piece of moose gut, and with my axehead I nail it to the tree a foot above the trap. To shield the bait from birds, I break off large twigs of spruce and stand them in the snow around the trap, but leave a small opening for the marten. Finally, I gather some fresh dry snow in the palm of my mitten and sprinkle it around the trap. Thinking that it will do, I put the dead marten into my basket, and go on my way, walking downhill into the cold bottom of Redmond.

×

The day passes, another hour, another mile. I walk, watching the snow, reading what is written there, the history of the tribes of mice and voles, of grouse and weasel, of redpoll and chickadee, hunter and prey. A scurry here, a trail ended there — something I do not understand, and stop to ponder. I find a trap sprung and nothing in it. I catch another marten, another male, so dark it is almost black. I am in luck today.

Already sunlight is fading from the hilltops. I look at my watch — it is past one, and I still have a good three miles to go. The air feels much colder here in this boggy creek bottom. I do not have a thermometer, but I judge it to be at least in the mid-thirties. There is some ice-fog in this valley, a thin haze in the air above the creek, and that is always a sign of cold and stagnant air.

The trail is slick in places where spring water has seeped up through the snow and frozen into a pale yellow ice. We call it "overflow" or "glaciering", and it is common here in winter. I watch carefully while crossing; the ice is firm, but where ice and snow meet, a little water sometimes steams in the cold air. I feel with my stick as I go, suspecting more water under the snow.

At times while traveling like this, absent in mind or misjudging the snow, I have broken through thin ice and plunged halfway to my knees in slushy water. I have always climbed out quickly, and with so many socks on my feet I have never been wet to my skin. All the same, there is some danger in it, and I do not want to walk the rest of a day with frozen socks and trousers and icy moccasins. Today I am careful, and only once, while crossing a short stretch of overflow, do I look behind me and see water seeping into my tracks from the thin snow.

×

Twilight comes on slowly across the hills and through the forest; there are no more shadows. I stop again in a stand of spruce above the crossing on Glacier Creek. I have been feeling hungry for some time, so I nibble a frozen cookie from my pack. I have no water to drink, but I remove one of my mittens, and with the warm, bare hand ball up some snow until it is ice, and suck it.

Five years ago we camped here in a tent while hunting moose. That was before we built the cabin, and before I had cut a trail across the creek. The four dogs were with us, tied here among the trees. It was late in the fall, and below zero much of the time, but the tent with its big canvas fly and sheet-iron stove was warm enough. The tent poles still stand here, ready for use, and our cache is still here, a rough platform built into the trees eight feet above me.

I put the three marten I have caught into a sack, tie it, and hang it from a spike high in the cache. I will pick them up on my way home.

I take my pack and go off downhill to the creek — there is no water on the ice, and I am across safely and dry. Then on through the woods and through the swamp, across a low saddle between two hills, tired now, and glad to be getting to the end of it. Fresh marten sign in the snow, and one more marten caught.

I am within half a mile of the cabin, when I find a lynx alive in a marten trap. It has not been caught long, the toes of one big forefoot barely held in the small steel jaws. The animal backs away from me, crouched and growling, its big tawny eyes fastened upon me, and its tufted ears laid back.

I take off my pack, approach carefully, and when I am close enough I hit the lynx hard on its head with my stick. Stunned, the animal sags in the snow. I turn the stick and hit it again with the heavier end, and strike it again, until the lynx sprawls and relaxes, and I am sure that it is dead. For so large an animal, they are easy to kill, but I wait to be certain — I do not want it coming alive in my hands.

Sure that it is dead, I release it from the trap. It is a big male, pale, and a choice fur. I hang the trap in a tree and shoulder my pack. Pleased with this unexpected catch, I drag the big lynx by one hind foot the rest of the way to the cabin, leaving a thread of blood behind me in the snow.

II

The cabin is hidden in a dense stand of spruce on a bench over-looking a small, brushy creek. The creek has no name on the maps, but I have called it Cabin Creek for the sake of this camp. The ground is perhaps 1700 feet in elevation, and from the cabin I can look up and see the clear slope of Banner Dome another thousand feet above.

With its shed roof sloping north, the cabin sits low and compact in the snow, a pair of moose antlers nailed above a window in the high south wall. There are four dog houses to the rear of it, each of them roofed with a pile of snow-covered hay. A meat rack stands to one side, built high between two stout spruces, and a ladder made of dry poles leans against a tree next to it. A hindquarter of moose hangs from the rack; it is frozen rock hard and well wrapped with canvas to keep it from birds. Just the same, I see that camprobbers have pecked at it and torn a hole in the canvas. Nothing else can reach it there, seven feet above the ground.

Nothing has changed since I was last here, and there has been no new snow. Squirrel and marten tracks are all around the cabin, and some of them look fresh; I must set a trap somewhere in the yard.

I leave the dead lynx in the snow beside the cabin; I will skin it later. I lean my walking stick by the door and ease the pack from my shoulders — I am a little stiff from the long walk, and it feels good to straighten my back. A thermometer beside the door reads 30 below.

I open the door, go inside, and set my pack down by the bunk. The cabin is cold, as cold as the outdoors, but there is birch bark and kindling by the stove, and I soon have a fire going. The small sheet-iron stove gets hot in a hurry; I watch the pipe to see that it does not burn.

As the cabin warms up I take off my parka, shake the frost from it, and hang it from a hook near the ceiling. The last time I was here I left a pot of moose stew on the floor beside the stove. Now I lift the pot and set it on the edge of the stove to thaw.

I will need water. Much of the time here I scoop up buckets of clean snow to melt on the stove. There is not much water in a buck-etful of dry snow, even when the snow is packed firm, and many

16

buckets are needed to make a gallon or two of water. But this year the snow is shallow, and it is dirty from the wind, with dust and twigs and cones from the trees around the cabin.

And so while the light stays I take a bucket and an ice-chisel, and go down to a small pond below the cabin. Under the snow the ice is clear, and in a short time I chop enough of it to fill the bucket. There is water under the ice, but I know from past use of it that the ice itself is cleaner and has a fresher taste.

Before going back up to the cabin I stand for a moment and take in the cold landscape around me. The sun has long gone, light on the hills is deepening, the gold and rose gone to a deeper blue. The cold, still forest, the slim, black spruce, the willows and few gnarled birches are slowly absorbed in the darkness. I stand here in complete silence and solitude, as alone on the ice of this small pond as I would be on the icecap of Greenland. Only far above in the blue depth of the night I hear a little wind on the dome.

I stir myself and begin walking back up the hill to the cabin with my bucket of ice. Before it is dark completely I will want to get in more wood. There are still a few dry, standing poles on the slope behind the cabin, and they are easy to cut. There will be time for that.

×

Past three o'clock, and it is dark once more. I am done with my chores. Inside the cabin I light a kerosene lamp by the window, and hang my cap and mittens to dry above the stove. The ice has half-melted in the bucket, and the stew is hot and steaming. I have eaten little this day, and I am hungry. I put on the kettle for tea, set out a plate, and cut some bread. The stew is thick and rich; I eat it with the bread and cold, sweetened cranberries from a jar beneath the table.

Fed and feeling at ease, I sit here by the window, drinking tea, relaxing in the warmth of the cabin. The one lamp sends a soft glow over the yellow, peeled logs. When we built this cabin I set the windows low in the walls so that we could look out easily while sitting. That is the way of most old cabins in the woods, where windows must be small and we often sit for hours in the winter, watching the snow. Now I look out the double panes of glass; there is nothing to see out there but the warm light from the window falling to the snow. Beyond that light there is darkness.

I get up from my chair, to put another stick of wood in the stove and more water in the kettle. I am tired from the long walk, and sleepy with the warmth and food. I take off my moccasins and lie down on the bunk with a book, one of a half dozen I keep here. It is Virgil's *Aeneid,* in English. I open the book to the beginning of the poem and read the first few lines. Almost immediately I fall asleep. When I wake up, it is nearly six o'clock; the fire has burned down and the cabin is chilly.

I feel lazy and contented here with nothing urgent to do, but I get up anyway and feed more wood to the stove. On my feet again, moving around, I find that I am still hungry — all day out in the cold, one uses a lot of fuel. So I heat up what remains of the stew and finish it off. Tomorrow I will cut more meat from the quarter hanging outside, and make another pot. What I do not eat, I will leave here to freeze for another day.

Having eaten and rested, I feel a surge of energy. I go outside to bring in the lynx, intending to skin it; I don't want to carry that heavy carcass home. The lynx is already stiff, beginning to freeze. I carry it in and lay it on the floor near the stove to thaw, while I make myself another cup of tea. When I can move its legs easily, I pull one of the big hind feet into my lap and begin to cut with my pocket knife below the heel where the footpad begins. The skin is stiff and cold under the thick fur as it comes slowly free from the sinew.

But soon in the warmth of the room I begin to see fleas, red fleas, crawling out of the fur. One of them, suddenly strong, jumps onto me, and then to the bunk. That is enough. I put down my knife and take the lynx back outdoors. I will leave it here to freeze, and when I come again the fleas will be dead. I am in no hurry about it, and I do not want fleas in my clothing and in my bunk. Already I begin to itch.

Outside, I leave the lynx in the snow once more, and for a brief time I stand in front of the cabin, to watch and listen. The cold air feels good on my bare skin. The stars are brilliant — Polaris and the Dipper overhead. Through a space in the trees to the south I can see part of the familiar winter figure of Orion, his belt and sword; in the north I see a single bright star I think is Vega. I hear an occasional wind-sigh from the dome, and now and then moving air pulls at the spruces around me.

What does a person do in a place like this, so far away and alone? For one thing, he watches the weather — the stars, the snow and the fire. These are the books he reads most of all. And everything that he does, from bringing in firewood and buckets of snow, to carrying the waste water back outdoors, requires that he stand in the open, away from his walls, out of his man-written books and his dreaming head for a while. As I stand here, refreshed by the stillness and closeness of the night, I think it is a good way to live.

But now the snow is cold through my stocking feet, and I go back indoors. I wash the dishes and clean the small table, putting things away for the night. I hang up my trousers and wool shirts, and hang my socks on a line near the ceiling. There is still some hot water in the kettle; I pour it into a basin, cool it with a cup of cold water from the bucket, and wash my face and hands. Having dried myself and brushed my teeth, I am ready for bed.

Lying on the bunk once more, with the lamp by my left shoulder, I pick up my book and try to read again. A page, and then another. My mind fills with images: a fire in the night, Aeneas, and the flight from Troy. I drowse, then wake again. I remember Fred Campbell lying on his cot in the Lake cabin that good fall many years ago, the Bible held overhead in his hand as he tried to read. And soon he was sleeping, the book fallen to his chest. The same page night after night. I was amused at him then, but older now I see the same thing happens to me. It is the plain life, the air, the cold, the hard work; and having eaten, the body rests and the mind turns to sleep.

I wake once more and put away my book. I get up from the bunk and bank the fire, laying some half-green sticks of birch on the coals, and close down the draft. Ice has melted in the bucket; there is plenty of water for the morning.

I blow out the lamp and settle down in the sleeping bag, pulling it around my shoulders. I look into the dark cabin, and to the starlight on the snow outside. At any time here, away from the river and the sound of traffic on the road, I may hear other sounds — a moose in the creek bottom, breaking brush, a coyote on a ridge a mile away, or an owl in the spruce branches above the cabin. Often it is the wind I hear, a whispering, rushy sound in the boughs. Only sometimes when the wind blows strongly from the south I hear a diesel on the road toward Fairbanks, changing gears in the canyon. And once, far away on a warm south wind, the sound of dogs barking at Richardson.

×

I spend another day at the cabin, taking my time. I loaf and read, cut more wood and chop some ice. I thaw and skin the one marten, and roll the fur in a sack to take with me; it will mean a pound or two less to carry, and more room in the basket. With the ladder and a block and tackle, I take down the moose quarter, unwrap it, and saw a piece of meat from the round. It was killed late, and is not fat meat, but having hung frozen for so long it is tender enough. The outside of the meat is darkened and dried and will need to be trimmed. I put the piece I have cut on a board near the stove to thaw.

In the afternoon I go up the creek to look at some snares I have set there. I find that nothing has come but one lynx, and he pushed a snare aside. It may have been the one I caught.

From the creek I climb a couple of miles up the ridge toward the dome. It is easy walking in the light snow, and here on higher ground there is bright sunlight and the air seems to be warmer. There is plenty of marten sign in the open spruce mixed with aspen, and I set two traps.

I mark the days on a calendar, drawing a circle around the dates. The calendar shows a ship, full-rigged in the old romantic style of the sea, hard-driven from Cape Horn, or following the trades homeward. This calendar comes from Canada, and bears the trade name of *John Leckie & Company, Ltd., Edmonton, Alberta. Marine Supplies and Hardware.* Three years ago I bought a whitefish net from them by mail, and now each year they send me a calendar. Since we have others at home, I bring them here. They look fine against the log walls, and brighten their place by the window.

I remember how we built this cabin, the many hours here, the long walks in the rain that turned into snow. I had the big wall tent pitched in the woods, near where the cabin is now, a cot to sleep on, and the small iron stove with its pipe stuck through a piece of sheet metal in the tent roof. I would come here from home in the afternoons, packing some food, lumber and tools. I worked on the cabin until dark, and slept overnight in the tent. Again the next morning, from the first light, I worked hard, trimming and fitting the logs, then walked home in the afternoon over the wet hills.

I worked from early August until mid-October, a few hours or a day at a time. Fall came early that year, and toward the end of it I was scraping frozen bark from the roof poles, determined to make a clean job of it. There was no dry sod for the roof, so we went to the creek to cut big batts of half-frozen moss and carry them up the hill one at a time. And finally we had a roof on the cabin, the door hung and windows fitted, and a fire in the stove.

That fall I shot a moose from the front of the cabin just at dusk. It was a long shot down into the flat below the hill, the moose only a dark shape in the frozen grass. Then came the work that evening and part of the next day, cutting the meat into quarters and dragging them up the hill to the camp. We hung the meat high on the rack I built that morning behind the cabin. We had a long walk home that afternoon in wet snow, carrying with us a chunk of the ribs, the tongue, the heart, the kidneys and liver. It was a hard fall, in many ways the hardest and poorest year I have spent in the north.

But the time and work was worth it, for here is the cabin now, snug and warm. No matter how long it stands here, it will always seem like a new thing, strange to come upon far in these hills at the end of a long hike, and to know we have built it.

I look around me, at the floor, at the walls, at the ceiling, the logs and poles. When the cabin was first built we had only hay for a floor, a deep bed of it spread on the moss. There was nothing to sweep or to clean, and each fall I brought in a few armloads of new hay to freshen the floor. But as cheery and rustic as it was, there were things about that hay floor I never liked. Frost was deep in the ground beneath the hay, and because the cabin went unoccupied for many weeks in winter, it was cold and damp to live in until the fire had thawed it. Mice and squirrels tunneled through the moss and into the cabin, and made a mess in the bedding. And so one spring before the trail went soft, I brought sledloads of lumber here. In August of that year I came and worked three days, putting in a proper floor. Now it is dry and warm, and the mice stay out. I sweep it now and then.

There is only the one room, eight feet by twelve feet, but it is large enough for a camp in the woods. The door opens west, and the two windows face north and south. Overhead I have cut a round hole in one wall for a vent, and fitted it with a metal lid. The peeled poles of the ceiling are still clean and bright yellow; smoke has not darkened them and the roof has never leaked.

Here at the back of the room I have built two bunks, one above the other, with a small ladder at one end to reach the upper. The table I eat from and the work table across the room are both fashioned from two-inch wooden pegs driven into auger holes in the logs. Boards are laid across the pegs and nailed in place. The few shelves are made in the same way. It is a simple means of making the essential furniture, and there are no table legs to get in the way underfoot.

Here and there I have driven nails and spikes into the walls; some odds and ends of clothing hung there, a few traps, a piece of rope. A .22 rifle is propped on a couple of spikes at the foot of the lower bunk. Behind the stove hang pots and washpans, and into one log by the door I have driven a 12 inch spike from which I hang the dog harness to dry.

There have been other winters here, not easy ones. I have come after a heavy snowfall, with the dogs dead-tired and me walking behind or in front of the sled, breaking trail. We were five or six hours getting here, the traps buried, something caught but hard to find in the snow. And then would come the journey home the next day over a soft, half-broken trail with a load of meat and three dogs; me again walking behind, steering, holding the snubline while the dogs pulled ahead.

Fifty years ago in the twilight of the goldrush, wagon roads and freight trails were still in use here. Though they are badly overgrown now and deeply rutted, I can still walk parts of them for a short distance; they go up the creek, across the divide and down Shamrock, to the Salcha River and Birch Lake, many miles from here. It is strange to think of it then, the country still busy with people coming and going, the dogs and horses, freight and men.

No one comes here now but Jo and myself, the dogs and us, the moose and the marten. Only once three years ago two men came to prospect with a Cat on Glacier Creek, two miles from here. They cleared a small piece of ground on the bench above the creek, but they found nothing there and did not come back. I am glad of that, I like having this country to myself.

I am living out a dream in these woods. Old dreams of the Far North, old stories read and absorbed: of snow and dogs, of moose and lynx, and of all that is still native to these unpeopled places. Nothing I have yet done in life pleases me as much as this. And yet it seems only half-deliberate, as if I had followed a scent on the wind and found myself in this place. Having come, I will have to stay, there's no way back.

The hunting and fishing, the wild fruit, the trapping, the wood that we burn and the food that we eat — it is all given to us by the country. The fur of this marten is lovely when held in the light, shaken so that the hair stands from the pelt. And meat of the moose is good to have: it keeps us fed and warm inside, and I pay no butcher for it. Yet I cannot trap and kill without thought or emotion, and it may be that the killing wounds me also in some small but deadly way. Life is here equally in sunlight and frost, in the thriving blood and sap of things, in their decay and sudden death.

It can be hard and cruel sometimes, as we are prepared to see it clearly. I put the beast to death for my own purposes, as the lynx kills the rabbit, the marten the squirrel, and the weasel the mouse. Life is filled with contradictions — confused and doubting in the heart of a man, or it is straight as an arrow and full of purpose.

I look at my hands and flex my fingers. They have handled much, done things I hardly dreamed of doing when I was younger. I have woven my nets with them and made my snares. I have pulled the trigger of my rifle many times and watched a bird fall or a moose crumple to the ground. And with these hands I have gone deep into the hot body of the animal, and torn from it the still-quivering tissue of lungs, heart, liver and guts. There is blood under the nails, dirt and grease in the cracks of the finger joints.

I have learned to do these things, and do them well, as if I'd come into something for which I had a native gift. And a troubling thought will return sometimes: having done so much, would I kill a man? I do not know. I might if I had to, in anger, perhaps, passion of defense or revenge. But not, I think, in the cold, judging light of the law. I have seen a war, a dead man floating in the sea off a Pacific island, and I was there. By my presence alone, I took part in many deaths. I cannot pretend that I am free and guiltless. Justice evades us; the forest with all its ancient scarcity and peril is still within us, and it may be that we will never know a world not haunted in some way by a return to that night of the spirit where the hangman adjusts his noose and the executioner hones his axe to perfection.

I put these thoughts away, and look out the window to the sunlit snow on the hillside across the creek. In this wilderness life I have found a way to touch the world once more. One way. To live the life that is here to be lived, as nearly as I can without that other — clockhands, hours and wages. I relive each day the ancient expectation of the hunt — the setting out, and the trail at dawn. What will we find today?

I leave some of my mankindness behind me for a while and become part tree, a creature of the snow. It is a long way back, and mostly in shadow. I see a little there, not much, but what I see will never be destroyed.

I may now always be here in these woods. The trails I have made will last a long time; this cabin will stand twenty years at least before it falls. I can imagine a greater silence, a deeper shadow where I am standing, but what I have loved will always be here.

*

Night, and the day passes. Evening, another pot of stew — rice and chunks of meat, dried vegetables, onions, a little fat, and spice for flavor. The weather holding steady, still 29 below. I continue to hear some wind on the dome.

I rise early on the morning of the third day, make my breakfast by lamplight. Oats and bread, some meat in the frypan. Might as well feed up, it will be another long day. I take my time this morning, dressing slowly, putting things away. I bring in more wood and stack it by the stove. Outside in the clear frost I hang the frozen lynx high on the rack; nothing will bother it there. Dawn comes slowly over the hills, lighting the snowy dome.

I pack my gear — the small axe again, a few traps. One marten skin to carry, three marten to pick up on the way. My pack will be as heavy as before.

The fire slowly dies and the cabin grows cool again. I fill a shallow pan with the remaining water and place it on the stove. It will freeze, and I will have water quickly the next time here. I put away my saw and the big axe; there is bark and kindling at hand when I come again. I close the door and latch it. I look around with care, at the cabin and the yard — everything is in place. I will be back in a week or ten days.

It is minus 24 degrees this morning; some thin clouds are forming, it may snow by evening. I take my pack and, stick in hand, set off up the trail toward Glacier Creek.

III

It is evening again, and I have come home by the river from Banner Creek. I came by another trail today, over the long divide between Redmond and Banner, another part of the country. It was hard walking in places; much of it is steep sidehill scraped and gouged by a Cat trail made many years ago, with several small springs and water under the snow.

I met with some wind on a high and open ridge where I could look east into the rose-grey morning sunlight. I felt too warm from climbing, and stopped to take the lining out of my parka. The wind came only now and then, not cold, a little loose snow blowing across the open trail.

Few traps and no marten there, but plenty of moose sign in the willows going down into Banner. One big red fox caught somehow in a trap set for marten, caught by the toes only, and not for long. He watched me as I came near, stretched out of the short chain, his eyes enormous with alertness and fear. I thought of trying to knock him out with a blow from my stick, so that I could free him from the trap and let him go. But I finally killed him, breaking his neck as I have learned to do. I put him into my pack with the others, tying him down, and took the trap with me.

I was close to Banner Creek, walking slowly on a straight and open stretch of the trail, when I came upon a set of wolf tracks.

They were soon joined by others, and I saw that two, possibly three wolves had come out of the dense, sloping spruce wood to the north, and finding my foot trail, had turned to follow it.

Thinking they might return in a few days, I set two heavy snares in that open place, a few yards apart from each other. I propped the nooses over my trail, supporting them with some brush cut from the woods close by and stuck down in the scant snow. I tried to make the sets appear as natural as I could, and looking at them afterwards from a distance, it seemed to me that they might work. Yet somehow I do not expect much from them; the wind may blow them down, or the wolves go around them.

I went on down Banner Creek, walking the old road between the spruce and the birch, the snow so light this winter it hardly fills the frozen ruts. A side path turning off into the woods brought me into a brushy flat where I keep an ancient and tilting cabin. I stopped there to build a fire in the stove and make some tea. My feet were sore from walking that hard trail in soft moccasins, and it felt good to take off the pack and rest for a while. The cabin is old and damp and does not heat well, but it is better than no camp at all.

Afterwards I searched in the brushy trails near the cabin where I have set snares for lynx. But I have caught nothing there this winter. Today one snare was missing; something had made off with it — what? The snow told me nothing.

In late afternoon I walked the last mile home along the Tanana, through the woods on the steep hillside between the river and the highway. The sun was gone, and light on the river, on the ice, a steely grey. Clouds were building a heavy darkness in the west. Sounds came to me along the river: water running somewhere out on the ice, a dog barking at Richardson. A car went by on the road, going to Fairbanks, going to Delta. People.

I sit here now, the long day over and the pack gone from my shoulders at last. My heavy clothing removed, moccasins hung up to dry, gloves and mittens drying on the rack above the stove. Half-sleepy, warmed by the fire, while Jo makes supper, and we talk. What happened while I was gone? Yesterday, today, the day before. A moose on the hill, water and wood, and no one came. The world is still the same, it will be the same tomorrow.

I am happy deep inside. Not the mind-tiredness of too much thought, of thoughts that pursue each other endlessly in that forest of nerves, anxiety and fear. But a stretching kind of tiredness, the ease and satisfaction of the time well spent, and of the deep self renewed.

Tomorrow, marten to skin and meat to cut. What else? It is two degrees below zero this evening. The wind is blowing.

IN RETROSPECT

U.S. LAND POLICIES AND HUMAN VALUES

Thomas LeDuc

OVER the past forty years I have pursued investigations in various branches of the field of United States history and in the course of doing so have been trying to determine some of the continuities and some of the interrelations in our national experience. This is not to claim that in any detailed way the study of our history can teach us how to react to the realities of the last quarter of the 20th century. You have doubtlessly heard the wry remark that we learn from history that we do not learn from history.

I am not qualified to outline a set of proposals for the future of Alaska and I shall not attempt to do so. My aim is to suggest some ways of thinking about the relations of man and resources.

Familiar to everyone is the image of the alien anthropologist studying a primitive and secluded culture. If one can imagine an anthropologist from another planet similarly dissecting American culture, what would he find most striking? I suspect that he would be instantly and overwhelmingly struck with two things: first, the vast power which a supposedly self-governing society has bestowed on its politicians and secondly, the materialism that is so deeply woven into the warp and woof of American society. Of the first I shall have occasion to speak as I go along.

For all of our spiritual pretensions, our assertions of commitment to the primacy of human values, we are unremittingly dedicated to the pursuit of the *goods* life rather than the *good* life. I am struck with the fact that as we enlarge our vision of equality and dignity of all people we articulate the vision largely in material terms like full employment and an abundant standard of living.

To implement our faith and reduce it to reality, we have always looked to government. When things go wrong we blame the politicians or demand that they come up with new programs. This reliance is not as new as some would have us believe, although obviously it is more pervasive than it was in the 19th century. But it is at least as old as 17th-century mercantilism. In the United States, the concept of government as a machine that could shape and stimu-

31

late the economy for the common wealth was elaborately spelled out by Alexander Hamilton almost two centuries ago and since then it has had a continuous vitality. As our perceptions of need change, the forms of response evolve, but it has always been true that economic depression is the terror and nemesis of American politicians. To avoid it or to end it they have always been partial to a program of borrowing in order to finance the inflationary spending that their political savvy told them would stimulate the economy, support prices and wages, and keep the voters happy. Those who think that deficit spending was invented in our own time simply do not know their American history.

In the 19th century politicians were able to borrow not only in cash, but to a vastly greater degree from the store of treasure held by the government in trust for the American people. That treasure was the public domain of undeveloped resources.

No nation in human history has had at its disposal such vast assets. By 1850 the federal government came to hold not just the sovereignty but the proprietary ownership of substantially all the resources west of the Appalachians and outside Texas. Today they are largely gone from public ownership and it is, I think, useful to see what we have done with them, how we made the decisions, and what ideas and values controlled the decisions.

One should recognize at the outset that the decisions were political decisions, that they flowed from the political process. Someone has counted columns in the Congressional Record and its predecessor reports and found that in the 19th century Congress spent more time talking about public-land policy than any other issue. One may add that the issues were thoroughly ventilated. When, therefore, Congress extended the public-land laws to a new territory, or failed to repeal a particular law, or failed to eliminate provisions that weren't working well, they had every reason to know what they were doing. In a sense, then, the question we shall be asking is simply: how good a job did democratic government do?

In asking that question one betrays his belief that it is conceptually possible to define what is sound in policy in terms objective and independent of the yield of the political process. I am not unaware that one school of political theorists argues that the only definition of "good" policy is the policy that emerges from the political process. One has difficulty in accepting that proposition for it seems to put one adrift with no chart and no compass.

The simple realities of proprietary ownership and political jurisdiction over the resources of most of the lower 48 states operated to confer on the American people plenary power to decide what should be done with them, and, good or bad, the decisions were made by chosen representatives. I emphasize this because some historians have attempted to explain the follies and failures of public policy in this, as in other respects as the result of perversions wrought by malign special interests. Now fraud and corruption and dishonesty there have been, but the candid historian must acknowledge that it does not explain the really big decisions. Is not our real problem to face the possibility that democratic goverenment really didn't do a very good job?

Did the disposal of the natural resources owned by the people operate to maximize their welfare, or does one see it used as a stock in trade by which politicians could attract votes?

In the century from roughly 1820 to 1920 most of the resources owned by the United States in the contiguous states passed into private hands and the value of the remainder was greatly diminished by private trespass and depredation. Behind this process of desocializing the public domain lay important assumptions, many of which were so generally held that they were rarely articulated.

First, was the idea that economic production is desirable and that resources should be put into production.

Second, was the idea that economic activity should rest with private enterprise and that government should play a minimal role in the making of decisions.

Third, was the idea that the farmer is the most beneficial member of society and should, therefore, be given favorable, or even preferential treatment. Central to this theme was not only a body of economic doctrine, but the value judgment that rural life is the fortress of the most important human virtues: thrift, industry, self-reliance, and providence.

If one can see in all of these themes symptoms of the ingrained materialism to which I earlier adverted, one can see, too, the implicit notion that wilderness was the embodiment of evil, to be tamed and subjected to man's uses.

In the light of these assumptions, it is easy to understand the course of resource-policy in the 19th century. What started as a rational, credible policy by which it was hoped the tillable land of the interior could be put into production on terms equitable to both society and the entrepreneur evolved over time into a grotesque anomaly which can be explained only as the fruit of political irresponsibility.

Without tracing in detail the unending revisions of the laws, one may offer some generalizations. The trend over time was to make it ever easier for individuals to get more land than they could develop or operate. After each depression, down to the Civil War, the statutes were so amended as to attract the impecunious to the West.

The result of this legislation — and of various extra-legal and illegal practices permitted by an easygoing government — was to stimulate the transfer of undeveloped resources to private hands. One cannot conscientiously say that it stimulated economic development or sustained human values. A host of impoverished migrants acquired title to land which they lacked the capital or know-how to develop or the labor to operate. There they lived in penury, waiting for some real developer to buy the land on terms profitable to the original entryman. What the land laws did, progressively and increasingly, was to foster the growth of an enormous class of petty speculators whose labor might better have been otherwise allocated. It was not they, by and large, who did the farm making, but those who came later and for the privilege paid more than Congress had intended.

The net political effect of all this was to gain the votes of those who first got the land. The homestead and preemption laws, together with the negligence of the land office, enabled squatters to get control of far more land than they could operate with the farm technology of the time. Even if they stayed to use a portion themselves, they could reap the capital gains from selling the excess.

Parallel with its policy of encouraging squatters, Congress throughout the 19th century was engaged in donating the public resources in support of what were certainly legitimate causes: education, transportation, migration, veterans' benefits, and a host of minor objectives like the production of salt. In effect, the land capital was being spent in lieu of cash appropriations by Congress. At a pace that increased as long as the supply lasted, Congress altogether gave away three-quarters of a billion acres. It was painless and popular, but the results were consistently so disappointing that one may question whether the asserted objectives were the real ones.

The new states, for example, got a quarter of a billion acres. From the day when Congress granted Ohio land to be used for support of public education, the states behaved irresponsibly in administering the trust, but Congress failed to introduce adequate restrictions and went on to enlarge the scale of donation. State governments were no less responsive to voter pressure than Congress. Only at the end of the century did some states begin to conform to the spirit of the law. Nebraska, having already sold her best land, decided to hold the rest and lease it on conditions that would preserve the resource values and at the same time return to the state, income commensurate with their value. By this policy the state has captured the long-term appreciation of value, expressed in higher rents, and still has an unimpaired resource of over a million acres.

Nebraska's program shows what could have been done on lands owned by the federal government. But it was in the very decade that the state was adopting sensible policies that the United States embarked on a policy, applicable only in that state, to quadruple the standard homestead and so accelerate the pace of petty speculation. Little of the land conveyed under that statute was ever used by the original grantees, but many of them found that they could sell it to persons who could not qualify under the law.

If one had time he could review the record of the huge donations to the states. Almost two-thirds of the area of Florida, for example, was given to the state. But it is easier to learn how much was given than what was accomplished by the gifts. As a recent beneficiary, perhaps Alaska can show a better performance.

By 1862 most of the tillable land in the humid region of the United States was gone from the public domain. In addition to selling land at fire-sale prices, the federal government had already given away several hundred million acres. Then in power was a party that had triumphed on a platform that promised free land to any settler. The homestead principle had already been tried on a limited basis in Florida, Oregon, and New Mexico and in every case it had served less as a way of promoting economic development than as a way of securing a valuable title which in a short time could be profitably sold. Possibly it was that experience that led politicians to recognize the political mileage that could be gained from applying the principle elsewhere.

The idea of free land had an enduring appeal that ultimately prevailed over the cautions of knowledgeable persons who pointed out some of the pitfalls. In the light of their warnings it is not surprising to find that more than half the homestead entries never went to patent, and that on the other half it was often hard to find any trace of occupancy. Under the act the government had no authority to determine the suitability of the person to take on the rugged life or to evaluate the suitability of the land. The hard fact is that many unqualified persons were allowed to take claims on land that should have never been opened to tillage farming. The act required the homesteader to build a house and to put in crops. Had the government enforced the law many fewer homesteads would have been patented. Government scientists warned that, in the subhumid region, farming would be risky and on the arid lands impossible, but that was precisely where most of the free land was. A neat symbol of this is the location of the homestead that has been identified as homestead number 1 and made a national historical monument. At the earliest possible moment under the law this claim was filed on land almost at the western boundary of the humid belt. To the west of it much of the land should have been left untilled under the protective native forage crops. Water was scarce; trees were scarce. The land, in a word, was unsuited to intensive agriculture.

It has been said that the government bet the homesteader that he couldn't last five years. It is easy to say that the homesteader risked nothing and lost no more. That pecuniary accounting leaves a lot unsaid. From a human viewpoint the Homestead Act was a cruel hoax that brought disaster to women and children and to the men tempted by what the politicians told them was a golden opportunity.

Concerning the Homestead Act, it is important to remember that in 1862 hundreds of millions of acres of undeveloped humid land were available to the farm maker. Under the easy laws of earlier years it had passed from public ownership and was being held for sale by those who had seen a bargain. Had the federal government been genuinely interested in economic development or in aiding the surplus farm population, it could have embarked on a program of development credit with which young couples of farm origin, with the skills and the will to farm, could finance the purchase of the livestock and implements and as much land as could then be farmed by a family. No one needed 160 acres, nor could he farm that much.

Long after it was completely evident that tillage farming could not succeed in the arid lands, Congress left the homestead act in force. Why it took Congress 70 years to face this reality I have never been able to understand. In the interval much land was homesteaded and then sold for cattle ranches. During those years the government would neither sell nor lease a quantity sufficient for a ranch. The man who had the capital and the knowhow to put the land to its highest and best use could not deal with the federal government but only with intermediaries: those like the states, the railroads, and the homesteaders to whom the government had given the land. Otherwise, he could run his stock on the public lands and hope he would not meet too many competitors.

The failure of the federal government to police the public lands in order to prevent overgrazing led to serious and often irreversible damage to that resource.

No less serious was the damage done by the wheat ranchers. The squatter had never scratched up much land; his chief crop was capital gains. But the wheat farmer plowed up enormous acreages that should have been left under grass for forage. If he owned the land he could misuse it if he chose. In doing so, he anticipated making more money on wheat than he could on cattle. So today we go on, producing twice as much wheat as we can eat, while livestock prices skyrocket. Meanwhile, we discover that permanent damage has been done to the land resource, for we find that it is extremely difficult to reseed these lands to the native forage crops.

Just as Congress failed until recently to formulate a rational policy for the grasslands still in its possession, so too until the 20th century it preserved the right to file a homestead on land suited only for forest crops. Most of the timberlands west of the Appala-

37

chians were unsuited for tillage agriculture and thus unsuited to the
land-disposal laws designed for farm land. But Congress failed to
recognize this reality. Stumpage or cutting rights could not be
bought; no adequate steps were taken to prevent theft by depredation; and no restrictions were imposed on lumbering practices on
land disposed of by the federal government, or held under unper-
fected claims. Here, as on the arid grasslands, those who were prepared to make the highest and best use of the land had to deal with
intermediaries who, in effect, were vested by Congress with certain
profit.

Happily, the net effect on the environment was negligible. Timber, after all, is a crop and in a properly harvested tract there is
nothing more offensive than in a field devoted to the growth of
wheat. One might wish that better practices had been followed in
cropping the timber, but except in limited, local situations the damage has not been great.

Time does not permit us to discuss in detail the federal policies
governing mineral resources on the public lands. Obviously a body
of laws supposedly designed to stimulate the creation of farms were
inappropriate for mineral lands, but Congress long neglected to de-
vise any other system. Characteristically, the problem of finding
and extracting the minerals was left to private initiative and one
cannot say that if it had been dealt with by government enterprise
any better results would have followed. In the light of what I shall
later say, it is interesting to note that the first mineral-land statute
was designed to stimulate the production of lead bullets for the
army.

The case of gold and silver is special. Because the precious met-
als lay on land that had not been surveyed they could not be purchased; and until long after most of the gold had been taken from
California, the government permitted anyone to take the ores from
public property. That the government then bought what it already
owned is only another way of saying that it offered high wages to
those who found and gathered its scattered possessions. This may
have been the best way to get that job done, but one may ask
whether it was worth doing, for the effect of this high-wage policy
was to siphon away from more productive occupations a host of

workers, most of whom never produced much with their labor in the gold fields.

Popular mythology regards our policies for the disposal of the public lands as calculated to advance the course of economic development. In defending the endless easing of terms on which any man could obtain a tract of the public lands, contemporary politicians were forever invoking the image of the frontiersman who performed a public service by making the desert bloom as the rose. But objective examination of the historical data leads one to question whether economic development was the actual objective rather than the argument advanced to justify a quite different goal. There is no doubt that the 19th as much as the 20th century was obsessed with the idea of economic development. Idle resources were as offensive as idle hands.

But if economic development was the actual goal, Congress pursued a strange course in stimulating it. It is a truism that the price of land was but a small part of the costs of farm making. Since few pioneers possessed the necessary capital, a rational policy would have been to lend them part of the total investment, and to sell the land on long-term credit. The experience of the land-grant railroads is here highly instructive. Since their business was transportation they had a genuine interest in promoting the development that would generate the traffic. What they found was that if they set low prices on the land they attracted speculators who did not develop the land but held it for higher prices. They were led, therefore, to put prices on their land at levels that would make speculation unpromising and development mandatory. Only a person serious about farming would pay those prices. To help him, the railroads supplied various aids and encouragements — low-cost loans, advice, and often free transportation for development purposes.

Had the federal government followed similar practices the pace at which the public land moved into private ownership would have been slowed. It is difficult to see what social loss would have thereby been incurred.

By the close of the 19th century most of the land resources in the contiguous states had passed from public ownership. It is to me interesting that precisely at that time the United States abandoned its historic foreign policy and embarked on the ill-starred adventures that have characterized the last seventy-five years. All through the 19th century we had steadfastly avoided involvement in international struggles outside North America. In 1898 we began to intervene in the internal affairs of Latin American countries. Simultaneously we took a position in the West Pacific that has produced continuous cost without visible gain. In 1917 we started the practice in intervening in struggles among European nations. World War I reeducated the American people to lessons learned during the Civil War. War is good for economic prosperity. The farmers had not seen such prices in the previous fifty years and non-farm workers enjoyed full employment at record wages.

Those lessons were still familiar when it became clear that despite the humanity of its impulses, the diversity and intensity of its efforts, the New Deal had failed to fulfill its promise of delivering us from the decade-long depression. We can see now that the New Deal went at the problem from the wrong end. The attempt to trigger recovery by fostering the scarcity of goods and services did not, and I believe could not, do the job. The capacity to produce and the capacity to consume were in reasonable balance, but output and consumption remained far below capacity. Raising milk prices while children weren't getting their daily quota, destroying food while children went hungry — such things contributed neither to a decent standard of living nor to economic recovery.

By processes that historians disagree about the United States found its answer to depression in Roosevelt's foreign policy. It worked so well that we have been slow in trying less destructive programs. As World War II approached its end, businessmen, labor leaders, and government officials recognized that the end of massive deficit spending for destruction entailed the likelihood of a depression of great severity. It was generally assumed that after the pent-up savings were dissipated in consumer spending that wartime shortages had denied, an acute shakeout would occur.

Our politicians failed to formulate a program that would sustain the high standard of living which our economy was capable of delivering, without resort to foreign policy as an instrument of domestic economic stimulus. Acknowledging that what we had done in World War II had in fact created new threats, they called for a new program of alliances and military spending. The nations that had been our enemies now became our friends, and vice versa.

Now when one takes an independent and fresh look at American foreign policy in the twentieth century, three things stand out clearly. (1) its necessity and utility stand largely on unsupported assertion. The politicians have failed to make a case for it. (2) the implementation of foreign policy has been used by the government as a make-work program. (3) to foreign policy we have allocated not only massive manpower but significant quantities of our natural resources, both renewable and non-renewable.

Let me elaborate on each of these points.

I have said that the politicians have failed to make a persuasive case for their foreign crusades. It rests largely on assertion supported only by emotional verbiage. The American people are easy to frighten with foreign ogres, and the politicians have exploited that fear. But stripped of its scare slogans, the case for insecurity doesn't hold water. Does anyone now seriously claim that it was crucial for the United States to go into Cuba and the Philippines in 1898, or to save one set of imperialist nations in Europe in 1917? Look, if you will, at the absurdity of our historic China policy. In 1900 we said that our goal was a free and independent China and in the 1940s we spent billions of dollars and scores of thousands of lives to get it. But no sooner had China become free and independent than we began to lament what we had done. Now that free and independent China is held before the American people as a prime danger, or at any rate it was until the most recent contradiction of our policy. Look, too, if you please at our behavior towards Russia. In World War II we were told that Russia must be rescued lest democracy everywhere fail. To the Soviet we sent all kinds of material aid and waged war on her enemies. We succeeded in the "Save the Soviet" operation only to hear, almost overnight, from Washington that it was all a mistake, that Russia, after all, was a great menace that must be confronted and contained with the power of massive retaliation, and that Germany must be protected from punishment for the slaughter she had wrought in Russia. Is it unfair to ask Washington to make up its mind?

One of the components of the protean psychology of scare is to claim that the survival of democracy in the United States is contingent on its preservation and extension everywhere on the globe. This unsupported allegation articulates an emotional bias that has led us into endless interventions in civil conflicts all round the globe. So far as they have been adversely viewed by American critics it has been on the ground that we are usually found intervening on the side of two-bit tyrants who are glad to have our help in their contests with rival tyrants. Cannot more fundamental questions be asked? Viewed objectively, does it really matter to us which set of tyrants runs Greece, or Southeast Asia, or some banana republic in Latin America? You will recall that with bipartisan planning and support in 1961 we launched an invasion of Cuba that failed. We have survived that failure as we survived the regime that we helped Castro dislodge. And if Castro is so evil, why are we now getting ready to sit down and live with him?

Since the days of Woodrow Wilson the assumption has been that with limited and brief inputs of men and money we can control the politics of other nations and the course of international relations. The evidence does not support that proposition. It suggests, rather, that there is no alternative to perpetual military occupation. Our forces have been in Korea and Germany for almost thirty years now, and no spokesman in Washington claims that those situations are any nearer to stability.

One may ask why the American people continue to support the basic concepts of American foreign policy and condemn only such grotesque applications as our adventure in Vietnam. If, as seems to be universally recognized now, the whole Vietnam intervention was a colossal blunder, why wasn't it so recognized ten years ago? If the architects of American foreign policy were there mistaken or incompetent, why should we have any confidence in what they tell us about other things?

To these sour questions the best answer that I can offer is suggested by the second point about the use of foreign policy.

For the last third of a century our biggest industry has been war, past and future. Whatever its functional failure as an instrument of stated policy, it has brought us full employment and prosperity. Government procurement of supplies from contractors and labor for its own civil and military employment have together supplied millions of jobs and billions of dollars in consumer spending. Every economist agrees that when we go off a war footing we go off a prosperity footings. So deep is our dread of depression that we refuse to think about the hidden costs of the present regime of the fallacious reasoning behind it.

You will agree that if someone goes down the street breaking store windows that he will create jobs for the repairmen. You will agree, also, that when the windows are replaced society will be no better off, that the labor expended in making and installing the glass will not give society a commensurate return, and that the labor of breaking and replacing could have been put to better use. One must ask whether this make-work fallacy doesn't underlie much of popular thinking about foreign policy. Should we not be asking what we have to show for the resources we applied to Europe in the 1940s or Asia in the 1950s and 1960s? Has our obsession with jobs so stifled our rationality and our concern for human values that we sacrifice millions of lives on its altar?

Our capacity to produce is so high that for thirty years we have been able to indulge in the make-work fallacy and still enjoy a high standard of living. That we have been able to do so should neither blind us to the costs nor inhibit our search for better alternatives.

Is it not time to apply a little common sense to our thinking about the relations of public policy and the standard of living?

It requires no elaborate calculus to demonstrate that with our current productive capacity we can, with the input of much less human labor than we are now expending, enjoy, or even raise, our present standard of living. This is not the undeveloped country that it once was. We have accumulated a vast capital for the production of goods and services, we have the technical and managerial know-how to use it. We have a skilled and literate labor force, we still have a great reservoir of renewable natural resources. So productive, for example, is American agriculture that with a farm work force of roughly 2.5% of our population we fill most of our needs in food and fiber and still have a lot to exchange abroad for the things we cannot produce. In the production of bituminous coal we have in fifty years reduced the input of human labor by perhaps 75% and production of other forms of energy are even less intensive of labor.

If these illustrations are representative, why do we need a work force of 75 or 80 million? If we are so productive, why is it that, to purchase the present standard of living, one and often two persons in a family are working the year round for forty or forty-five years?

The answer, of course, is that they are buying much more than that standard of living. They are buying a lot of foreign policy, a lot of that made work of which I was earlier speaking. As consumers and as taxpayers they are footing the cost. The individual is conscious of the taxes he pays himself; he is certainly less aware that as a consumer he is helping pay the taxes of those who sell to him or work for him. Last year, for example, General Motors paid $3 billion in taxes and everyone who bought their products contributed to that payment.

Now it will be said that if we reduced our expenditure for military services and foreign aid that we would precipitate unemployment. Of course. But that superficial conclusion begs the main question. The real question is whether we are going to allocate resources to the production of goods and services for consumption or for destruction. If we answer that question in favor of the consumer, we will find that we can reduce the total input of human labor, and diffuse the excess so as to permit greater leisure for the entire work force. Before we can achieve that objective we must cope with the ethic, almost universal and deeply ingrained in our mores, that says that a man *should* work 100,000 hours in a lifetime. Leisure is not a dirty word but rather a humane concept that must be freed of the lingering stigma of immorality. We no longer accept the sixty-hour week as the norm nor will we put up with the practice of employing little boys and girls in coal mines. Within my own lifetime both of those realities have disappeared and I see no reason why we cannot go on from there to shorter spans of work years and other modes of reducing labor. If we no longer accept 18th-century standards it is because we don't have to.

The tasks of reordering our distribution of manpower and other resources will require that we summon human intelligence to our aid. *That* resource we have in abundance. Whether we shall use it is far less certain.

It is notorious that American society has been readier to apply human intelligence to material and technological problems than to solving social problems. We can send missiles half way round the world, but we seem to have difficulty in recruiting honest policemen. We can put men on the moon, but we seem to have difficulty in teaching kids to read; modern medicine can perform wonders, but ignorance or poverty deny its services to many citizens.

So far as government has failed to solve our problems, we tend to blame the politicians, for perhaps subconsciously we recognize that they are identical. Government is not an automaton, performing mechanically, but an aggregation of human beings. Because politicians hold power, we tend to think of them as leaders. But are they, really? Politicians respond to their perceptions of what the voters want, and, in that sense, are followers. Politics, after all, is a mass medium, performing similarly to other mass media. The patrons get what they want, or what the performers think they want. If the people make it clear that they want peace, one can be sure that they will get it, and if they want resource policies that embody human values, they will get them.

Mass demands for particular changes are, as any politician can tell you, often ephemeral. Occasionally they last long enough to achieve permanent results. In the history of every such movement can be seen a long-term process in which some new insight is gained by a tiny but vigorous and dedicated minority. From their missionary work eventuates a body of persons sufficiently large or powerful as to command attention. Eventually, politicians take up the cause and get it formulated in public policy. In our own time we have seen this take place with the crusade against pollution of the environment. Less than a generation ago a handful of persons began to talk about pesticides and radiation. A campaign that originally had very limited goals has expanded to the point where the federal government has begun to enforce laws that had been dead letters for seventy-five years, and even to clean some of the pollution created by federal agencies.

More important, perhaps, we have come to recognize that the natural environment is more fragile than we had known. That perception has taught us that there is much that we still don't know about the world that our children must occupy, and this humbling thought teaches us anew that it is only man's vanity that announces

45

that we conquer nature rather than use our intelligence to learn how to live with it.

All this offers, I hope, a cheerier note on which to conclude.

The political process is not innately vicious or hopelessly irresponsive. Those who believe that it is, or was, excessively responsive to material values must recognize that it was probably conforming pretty closely to the model. Those who feel that it should be more attuned to human values must face the fact that their task is that of educating and mobilizing that power which we know commands the deepest and most enduring respect of the politicians: public opinion.

THE ALASKA NATIVE CLAIMS SETTLEMENT ACT IN PERSPECTIVE

Monroe E. Price

THERE is a rhythm to Indian policy in the United States, a strongly stated program or statute followed by a period of weakening commitment and direction. In one sense, it is the periods of decay that are interesting and typical; indeed, it is endurance through successive such periods that provides much of American Indian political culture, so much of its character and special quality of cynicism amidst seeming cooperation. Such periods of indifference are characteristic of federal relations with the Alaska Natives. But it is not the intermediate periods that are always of interest, though they may be the truer hallmark of federal policy. Instead, it is the main themes of Indian policy themselves, including the most recent efforts to develop a national program and effective national legislation.

The function of analyzing Indian policy and the Alaska Native Claims Settlement Act here is not only to determine the substantive program of the government toward indigenous people at a particular moment. Rather it is to look at the law as the "skin and feeling of a society." The idea is that statutes relating to Indians can be analyzed not only for their operative significance, but also because of the way in which they betray, or, more subtly, objectify a community's sense of its goals and ideals.

Why is this so? Why should legislation respecting Native people be so important as a benchmark of the changing thinking and consciousness of a dominant society? Architects of Indian policy often have little direct familiarity with Native American realities. It is the idea of the Indian, perhaps, rather than what may be the more pedestrian facts of Indian life, that constitutes the engine for reform and change. Legislation which captures that idea may be more likely to gain a national constituency. Legislation that is in conflict with the prevailing idea of what is good and proper in fulfilling the idea of an Indian in American society is more likely to falter. Of

47

course, there then becomes a relationship between subsequent behavior and the legislation itself. The federal administrators, particularly those in positions of leadership, become responsible and successful based on their molding of behavior to the legislative ideal.

But where does the ideal arise, if not from actual experience with the problems of Indian existence? These ideals change from generation to generation, from decade to decade, but not because of changes in Indian actualities. There is a different source and I should like to suggest what it might be. While thousands of Native Americans are obviously affected by Indian legislation, sometimes critically and adversely, what is often the subject of the legislation is the creation of the romantic ideals of the public and the legislature. The question reduces itself, then, to a search for the source of that extension of imagination, the source of American ideals for Native Americans where actual experience itself is not the basis for public policy.

It is possible that, to some extent, the dominant society sought for Indians within its midst a role which it projected as the ideal for all within the community. At a time when the American character was best represented by the independent farmer developing his small farm, that became the legislated model for the Indian. From time to time, this source for Indian legislation is important, namely the perhaps unconscious desire to impose upon the Indian what collectively is perceived to be the best in terms of character and role as that is perceived collectively.

In an initial stage, the nation may have been dealing with an Indian reality. At that stage, the source for a legislative mandate was a set of problems, a need for the settler society to cope, to define its own place on the continent and its relationship to the aboriginal people. But after an initial period of rough equality of strength and some respect in the 17th and 18th centuries followed by a stage of combat and revulsion, there is a more stable and extensive period of dominance accompanied by romanticism. The society, nostalgic, recreates a past which may or may not have existed. Sometimes the romanticism may not be wholly respectful; indeed, it may attribute characteristics to the lost culture largely to contrapose the ideal with the seemingly more abject reality. The romanticism has a kind of corrosive impact. It instills in the dominant society a sense of guilt and desire for remediation. It portrays the indigenous people as a group desperately in need of assistance and greatly in need of the help and counsel of the dominant group.

Out of this romantic view comes, in part, the cyclical programs for reform, the rhythmic schemes. The more remote from the initial period. the greater the likelihood that legislation was built on perceptions of Indian reality and distant moralizing about what the proper course of Indian society should be. To the extent that facts and personal familiarity with Indian needs were not the source of Indian-related legislation, a kind of moral sense, derived from the majority's own musings about the ideal society, became a dominant force. And this moral sense frequently was accompanied by another force: for the history of the 19th and 20th centuries can be perceived as the general and steady opening of resources for consumption and use by the dominant society. The various refinements from period to period are of little consequence. What persists is that land, minerals, rights of way, oil and gas — all these are made available when and as needed by the dominant society.

These two perceptions — one looking at the idea of the Indian in American society and the other looking at the exploitation of resources by the non-Indians — are worth examining in terms of periods in American history, in terms of dealings with Indian people, and in terms of the conceptualization and implementation of federal legislation. They are clearly worth examining when studying the Alaska Native Claims Settlement Act.

This process did not begin with the 20th century. Its roots extend into American history as far back as general settlement and conquest can reach. Toward the mid-19th century, the policy of isolation held sway. The function of the federal government was to retain special islands of Indian culture, free of intervention and intrusion by the white settler. The non-intercourse legislation was the monument of this policy. At first the islands were located in the midst of the white cultures — in Georgia, in Mississippi, along the Eastern seaboard. But as the settler culture became too virulent, the principle of non-intercourse could not be maintained together with the principle of retention of ancestral lands. As a consequence, the policy of removal was emphasized. The great Indian cultures could and should remain, and the policy of isolation should be retained as well; but the Indians would have to remove to the outer bounds of the American society so that the impetuousness of the settler could be accommodated.

By 1887, as domination and romanticism began to mark the end of the period of conquest, the first major assimilative model of American federal policy was enshrined. The Dawes Act, or the General Allotment Act, provided that individual Indians should obtain 160-acre agricultural tracts, and with them the right to participate in the political process. To become a farmer was the American ideal; that was what had made the country great. Now the Indian was to follow in the ideal American's image. The civilizing quality of the farm was to be the antidote to the disease and decay that followed from conquest.

The General Allotment Act is generally agreed to be a disaster by almost every measure except for the number of acres taken out of Indian ownership. The civilizing capabilities of the legislation were not only misguided but ineffective. Yet the Act lingered as a major aspect of federal policy for almost half a century, and its effects are with us yet. Like all good federal Indian legislation, the Dawes Act was clearly a product of dual influences. The Indian Rights Association, the 19th century well-meaning reformer, was leagued in a sense with the dispossessors. The businessmen of the West realized that allotment of Indian lands would mean that they would be intimately marketable; if the lands could be sold, they would be. Instead of great masses of reservation land, drawing from the tax base, not supporting good settler families that contributed to the economy, there would be individual plots; and the Indian culture, to the extent it remained, would give way to the settler.

But the reformer liked the law too. The reservation was "in the nature of a school," as a judge said in an early Indian case. The reservation Indians were gathered there in the care of the superintendent to learn the lessons of American culture and to graduate into the mainstream of American society. For these reformers, the lesson of the collectivized reservation was not the proper one. It was critical that the reservation curriculum be revised so that the proper instruction was inculcated into the Indian wards. Allotment provided that lesson. Instead of the dangers of collective economy, each person or each family now would learn to fend for himself. For each allottee, the benefits of hard work could be readily realized. To be a hard working farmer in a collective setting might be self-defeating, particularly when the federal benefits provided an alternative. To be a farmer in an allotment scheme would be readily perceived as a desirable and virtuous life.

This was the theory. Alas, it failed. Or at least it failed for the reformers.

In the 20th century, there have been other great assaults. The Indian Reorganization Act of 1934 sought to recapture what was lost in the 19th century and what was virtually destroyed by the General Allotment Act, namely, the group identity of a reservation or band of Indians. Aghast at the nihilistic qualities of government paternalism and forced land reorganization in the previous half-century, the New Deal sought to reestablish the collective. The objective was to build a strong tribal government, one that had the power to make effective decisions for the benefit of its membership.

This was a noble experiment, but it endured scarcely a decade. World War II provided a hiatus; and in the post-war era, the national consciousness was too egalitarian, too strong and proud to countenance the rather ethnic-oriented, separatist tendencies of the 1930's. The New Deal could applaud regionalism. It could provide through its pluralistic programs support for particular cultures in the American society. The National Industrial Recovery Act proceeded on the assumption that each individual industry could govern its own affairs. In the arts the special and disparate crafts and cultures of communities across the nation were supported. It was in this context that the genius of the Indian Reorganization Act must be appreciated.

The post-war era had far more prosaic goals. Refrigerators and cars for all constituted more of the American consciousness. And for the Indian there was an equivalent, the policy that by the 1950's became labeled *termination*. "Equality" in the most mundane sense became the watchword. People should not be different; indeed, it was probable that they did not want to be different. To be sure, federal money should not be spent that would preserve and prolong cultural differentiation. Rather funds should be expended that would facilitate cultural integration. Indeed, the same national higher spirit that struck down the "separate but equal" policy in public education would find it palatable to support elimination of the reservation system. What was prized in the 1930's could easily be seen, in the 1950's, as a regressive and un-American program.

As with the General Allotment Act, the termination programs have proved to be failures. They were to be a complete solution, in the sense that the programs would be self-liquidating. At the commencement of termination, there would be a given number of Indian persons entitled to see themselves as a part of a separate culture, partaking as well of the guardian-ward relationship. At the end of the termination program, there would be none or few Indians remaining in that condition. They would have removed to the urban areas or otherwise dispersed into the fabric of American life.

That has been the summum bonum for one stream of American reform. But it has not worked. The termination program led to some dissolution of Indian community life, but it was not potent enough to reduce the size of the remaining Indian collective societies.

Undoubtedly, the termination program, had it continued unabated, would have reached its goal. But in the 1960's and 1970's the consciousness of the nation seemed to change. Here the time becomes so close that is is difficult to ascertain the quality of transformation; it is not yet clear what the new and dominant motif may be or whether the programs, while appearing new, are really continuations of the trend set in the 1940's and 1950's. The creation of the Office of Economic Opportunity was, it may be said with some certainty, a major transforming event. Its funds and its policy of maximum feasible participation of the subject populations in the management of their programs clearly enunciated a return to the policies of the 1930's, the strengthening of the collective or tribal entity. The Bureau of Indian Affairs was drastically reduced in influence. The concept of advocacy, particularly the power of submerged groups to gain representation and use the power of newly defined rights, became part of reservation culture as it did the culture of the urban poverty areas. And the entire focus of federal funds changed as well. Where the financial incentive in Indian policy in the 1950's was to encourage Indians to leave the reservation to obtain jobs in urban areas, substantially greater federal funds were used to create an abundance of new employment opportunities on the reservation; and for the first time there were many jobs that were at the executive level. These jobs made it possible and legitimate to seek economic security as well as leadership in reservation affairs.

Where does the Alaska Native Claims Settlement Act fit in this history? The hallmark of the legislation is the corporate nature of the structures created and the spectacular embrace of corporate ideology. If the General Allotment Act of 1887 had the small farmer as its ideal and goal for the Indian family, and Alaska legislation has the corporate shareholder as its model. The General Allotment Act was not successful; as a consequence of the delay by Bureau personnel and the reluctance of certain tribes, Indian allotments were limited to a marked, rather than a pervasive influence on Indian lands. Not so the Alaska Settlement Act. By legislative stroke, the Congress converted all Alaska Natives into members of the corporate world, receivers of annual reports, proxy statements, solicitations, and balance sheets. The Native received a shotgun initiation into the American mainstream.

The ardor with which this original conversion has been received is testimony to its ideological force in our society. Village entities, for example, could, under the Act, organize as profit or non-profit corporations. Of the over 200 village corporations formed under the Act, not a single one initially filed papers as a nonprofit corporation, notwithstanding tax and other benefits that might have resulted from the choice of the nonprofit form. It is possible that there was a lack of information on the choices available. But it is also possible that the persistence of the profit motif in the Act, in its justification and in the resultant planning meant that retention of the for-profit form was, itself, perceived as an aspect of maturity of development. The assets transferred by the bill, one billion dollars and 40 million acres of land, are for the most part transferred to the twelve regional corporations and two hundred village corporations within Alaska. Each of the more than 60,000 enrolled Natives holds 100 shares in the regional corporation. The corporations are incorporated under Alaska state laws and are administered in accordance with the state's corporation statutes.

Aside from the symbolic differences, there are of course quite important actual differences between the tribe as paradigm and the corporation as paradigm for the organization of indigenous people. The major distinction relates to governance. The essence of a tribe is its existence as a political entity. How much authority the tribe may have is often open to question. The tribe, amorphous, ill-defined, subject to competitive pressures by other governments, may have difficulty asserting power to zone, to tax, to define criminal conduct and assess penalties for violations. There may be ambiguities in the authority over non-Indians or non-members or members that are not within the political boundaries of the tribe. But the essence of a tribe is its legitimate claim to some political authority. By choosing the corporate form, Congress has negated this claim to political authority. A corporation is an owner of assets and a manager of assets. It has no authority over personal conduct or behavior and, without specific statutory aids, has no governing power to control what kind of development or subsistence activity occurs within its sphere of influence.

The Native corporations, as established, still retain some of the vestiges of governance. The very titles of the corporations, particularly the village corporations, imply some faint remnant of governance. In the Arctic Slope area, there has been formed an organized borough, with governing authority under state law, whose boundaries coincide with a virtually all-Native population, so that there is some symmetry between the Arctic Slope Native Corporation and a true political entity. At this stage, the perceptions of the Native corporations include the feeling that they are quasi-governmental, that they are concerned with the future of the state and the fate of their stockholders in a way that is closer to political entities than it is to private corporations. Finally, through lobbying in Juneau and Washington, through their impact on the political process, the Native corporations seek indirectly to have some of the effect of a government on the future of the state.

A second major conceptual difference between a tribe and a corporation as paradigm relates to immunity from state law. Since the end of the 18th century, one of the hallmarks of tribal status has been the immunity of tribal lands from the imposition of state law. In terms of land use, the central aspect of this immunity has been the lack of application of state and local property taxes and the absence of the authority to zone. There have been degrees of immunity that have existed as a consequence of legislation, of judicial decision or of random practices. But always, as part of the essence of the nature of a tribe, there has been the notion of immunity from state law.

The Native corporations have limited immunity from state and local property taxation for a period of years and only under the circumstance that their land is not leased to third parties or developed (there may be, as always, ambiguities in the application of that term). Otherwise their operations and their properties are conceptually as subject to state laws as any other corporate entity within the state. There will be modifications as the corporations seek to interpose Indian Reorganization Act councils and as the state and federal government provide special exemptions from taxation or for subsistence purposes. But the essence of the distinction persists.

An exceedingly important, but ill-understood distinction between tribe and corporation as paradigm relates to the rights of the members against the central entity. A tribe is not only a political authority with governance powers, but it also has extraordinary immunity from actions by members that may weaken the authority of the tribe. As a consequence of Supreme Court decisions interpreting the United States Constitution, it has been held that a tribe is neither a state nor an agent of the federal government for determining whether individuals have rights to be protected against tribal acts which would otherwise be declared discriminatory. Furthermore, the Indian Civil Rights Act, which was passed by Congress to establish certain rights of individual members against the tribe, has been held not to confer jurisdiction upon state or federal courts to determine whether a violation has occurred. As a consequence, a tribe may be able, free of federal judicial interference, to deprive individual members of the right to vote, to infringe upon their free speech rights, to decide that elections to determine the makeup of the governing entity will be extremely rare.

Stockholders in the Native corporation have much more piercing and effective rights against the governing entity of the corporation. Alaska Native corporations are governed by Alaska state law, and all the protections furnished to stockholders in non-Native corporations apply. As a consequence, the individual shareholder has rights to disclosure, to notice of Board meetings, to attendance at annual meetings and other similar rights. The capacity of the Board to modify such rights is governed by state law. More important, the shareholder, under Alaska state law, has specific remedies in state court if he or she feels that management or the Board of Directors has taken an action that violated a duty to the corporation. Proxy fights can, and have been, waged. There may be frequent efforts to hold special meetings of the shareholders, empowered to displace the Board of Directors and enlist new management. In terms of stability, this means that a Native corporation management may have less assurance of its tenure than a politically established leadership of a tribe. This is particularly true because the Congress, by amendment to the Native Claims Settlement Act, removed the Native proxy fights from the protection and stewardship of the Securities and Exchange Commission.

There is a fourth difference between corporation and tribe as paradigm that is of critical importance in understanding the distinction. Concomitant to a tribe's authority to govern is its power to act, with particularity, to serve the individual needs of its subjects. A tribe can determine that certain of its members should have low cost housing or special loan programs or individual health services all based on their needs for such programs and their incomes. It is not clear that a Native corporation under the Alaska law has that leeway. A corporation which used its revenues to help poor shareholders at the expense of wealthier ones might be open to a shareholder's action rather than to praise for progressive redistribution policies.

This constraint is of fundamental importance. There may be those who look to the Native corporation to serve, in complex and creative ways, the needs of their shareholders. And it would be superb if they did so. But there is the fear, which may substantially affect the decisions of corporate officers, that business judgment rules will be brought to bear upon their actions. And groups of shareholders, anxious to obtain control, or at least obtain what they perceive to be fair, will attack conduct which is discriminatory, even beneficially so.

56

A fifth distinction between the tribe and the corporation relates to the power to dispose of property. To the extent that a tribe is a government, governmental considerations attach to its own decision to dispose of property held in common. To some extent, there is an attitudinal barrier to disposing of tribal property even if the tribe is legally permitted to do so.

Under the Native Claims Settlement Act, one of the very specific achievements was the removal of any barrier against sale of corporate land. No Secretarial approval is necessary. The land is held by the Native corporation in fee simple so that the managers of the corporation can enter into whatever transactions, consistent with corporate policy, they deem valid. For a period of ten years, regional corporations have the power to review the sale of land by village corporations within their region. But the right of review does not automatically include any veto right; furthermore, it is not clear that the inclination of the regions or the villages or the extent to which the federal government patented land to the village corporations yielded a right of review that would be frequently exercised.

A special corporate attribute of the Act is the enhancement of intergroup rivalries. By virtue of the intricacies of the Act, very often village corporations will be pitted against the region and the region will be pitted against other regions.

Finally, there is the right to ongoing federal benefits. The Alaska Native Claims Settlement Act does not, by its own terms, purport to sever Alaska Natives from any special federal programs. And there is no sign that for the average shareholder there is the kind of improvement in life that would suggest the lack of need for federal benevolence. That said, however, there is an aesthetic and constitutional sense in which the existence of tribes as paradigms, as compared to corporations, is more hospitable to the continued receipt of certain federal benefits. From an aesthetic perspective, there are undoubtedly those who think that Alaska Natives have now been given a dowry and sent off to succeed or fail. They are not like tribes where there is a continued federal interest in fostering self-government. From a constitutional sense, the question is whether benefits that are addressed specially to Natives are racial or tribal in basis. The most recent Supreme Court case, dealing with employment preferences for Indians in the Bureau of Indian Affairs, seemed quite pointedly to rest on the Bureau's role in governing tribes. To the extent Natives are not part of self-governing entities, there may be challenges to their inclusion in Indian-specific programs.

In a sense, the gospel of capitalism has gripped the leadership of the regional corporations just as in another day, another kind of gospel was introduced for its educative and assimilative influence. The profitmaking mandate has become a powerful vision, a powerful driving force.

The corporate structure and the financial responsibilities under the Act have another consequence. It must change the characteristics of leadership. This is certainly only a hypothesis, but the construct of values that were respected in the historic Native village will change. The corporate executives will be those who are willing to forego subsistence activities, to place a higher priority on board meetings than on salmon fishing, and to spend time talking to lawyers and financiers and bankers rather than the people of the villages. It is possible that there will develop a leadership cadre in the Native corporations that will become somewhat removed from the shareholders. The Native corporations, in this sense, will approximate other large businesses and that management will, more and more, be separated from ownership.

I have concentrated on the Alaska Native Claims Settlement Act in terms of its reformist aspect, namely the imposition of the corporate imprint on Native life in the state. But there is the other theme in the history of Indian legislation that is important here as well, namely the theme of opening resources for non-aboriginal use and development. The Settlement Act fits within the tradition of much of Indian policy because it quiets title to land in the state. While it reserves ten percent of the land for Native ownership, the legislation makes it clear that there is no continuing encumbering aboriginal title to the remainder of the land. Furthermore, the legislation, because of its lack of limitation on sale or lease of land, essentially was thought to open the land for development.

Passage of the Act was and still is looked at as a technique for placing large parts of the state in private hands. Perhaps out of stereotypical perceptions, the non-Native expectation seems to be that the lands involved will only be temporarily in Native ownership.

The Act even more clearly unlocks much of the mineral wealth in Alaska. There would have been no Native Claims Settlement Act of the present magnitude had it not been for the intense interest of the oil companies in its passage.

The Native Claims Settlement Act is the clear descendant of the earliest American approaches to Indian policy. Native occupancy is undisturbed until there is pressure for Native lands.

There are many who hailed the Alaska Native Claims Settlement Act as a great departure in the history of the dealings between the settler population and the Indian minority. The Act may still prove to be a great step forward. But for now the conclusion must be that the Act has its antecedents, and its relationship to the history of Indian law is clearer than its place outside that history.

TOWARDS AN ALASKAN LAND ETHIC

Walter B. Parker

EVEN the greatest recluse or lover of the wilderness at some time feels that need for contact with other humans and for complex social relations that can only be found in an urban environment. But too many cities repel too many of their inhabitants. They have become unlivable.

Land planner Ian McHarg has said: "There are cities that produce more stimulus and delight than can be borne, but it is rare when they are products of the industrial revolution or its aftermath. If we can create the humane city, rather than the city of bondage to toil, then the choice of city or countryside will be between two excellences, each indispensable, each different, both complementary, both life-enhancing." McHarg points out the importance of an attractive hinterland to the urban environment and the complementary relationships of regional and urban land planning. In Alaska, most of our communities are still surrounded by relatively unspoiled land.

When I think of cities and towns that produce "stimulus and delight," I think of San Francisco as it was thirty years ago. The difference between the San Francisco of yesterday and today is not primarily in the city. It is in the surrounding regions where some of the worst examples of American suburban planning have desecrated the Santa Clara Valley and overrun the hills of Marin County.

In contrast, Vienna, one of my favorite cities, has retained its unique spirit, the same spirit that has provided the stimulus for Freud, Mozart, Beethoven, and countless others despite the dreary starving times of the 1920's, the barbarities of National Socialism, and bombings near the end of World War II. The blythe Viennese spirit must depend in part on the Vienna Woods that largely surround the city. These woods are little changed from the days of Strauss, the Elder.

Citizens should define their city and recognize it for what it truly is. Definition is the first and most important step in urban planning.

Cities fill three general roles: as service centers for environs, as transportation centers for the distribution of people and goods, and as manufacturing, education, and recreation centers. For any given city, the degree of importance of these roles is important to recognize. Not to recognize the major role of a city can result in some strange priorities, such as setting aside large tracts of land in industrial zoning in cities which have no particular reason to expect any industrial development.

To determine what kind of city we really live in, we can examine two useful planning models. Constantine Doxiadis has developed a system of units ranging from the individual man to the world city or ecumenopolis. These units interact with five elements that make up the city — nature, man, society, shells, and networks.

Within each element are several subgroups. In nature, they are environmental analysis, resource utilization, land use and landscape, and recreation and tourism. Under man, they are physiological needs, safety and security, affection, belonging and esteem, and self-realization, knowledge and esthetics. Man is the web that binds all parts together into a synthesis of physical setting and biological relationships to create the city.

Popular today are the land use theories of Ian McHarg, where terrain slope, soil conditions, ground cover, and climate are brought together to determine the best use of land and the population density it can be expected to comfortably support under different urban conditions. McHarg's theory is fundamentally to "design with nature" and not to try to overcome natural obstacles through massive earth moving or drainage projects. He seeks in this way to achieve maximum urban efficiencies and economies in a happy and pleasant setting.

The administrator of the Federal Environmental Protection Administration said recently: "It is up to us to demand environments which ennoble man and amplify his potential instead of destroying it. Once we have understood that housing, transportation, population control, industrial zoning, pollution abatement, wildlife protection, energy planning, recycling of resources and outdoor recreation are all part of one Gordian package, we can free ourselves from the dictatorship of laissez-faire." It is this urban laissez-faire that destroys a community through the conversion of pleasant areas into scenes of ugly squalor. Controlling just two of the urban elements, land and buildings, can require all our care. Such laissez-faire also keeps a community divided with constant confrontation between those whose primary concern is the livability of the city and those who mostly regard it as a place in which to maximize profits. Only stable local government institutions that provide security to the family and neighborhood, while maintaining the necessary economic climate to provide jobs, can resolve the problem. Some communities succeed. For others time runs out as it has for Gary, Indiana; San Jose, California; and other cities that tried to do without parks, boulevards, and other amenities.

Too many communities assume that having a strict, enforced zoning ordinance will solve their land use problems. In reality, zoning is but a small part of urban planning, and if enforced too rigidly it can do great harm by maintaining barriers to communication and to desirable changes in lifestyles.

In Anchorage, the zoning ordinance is very strict about animals in residential areas, so strict that, as a practical matter, only dogs can be kept outside. These restrictions keep families from acquiring ponies as pets, yet in many ways ponies are more conducive to amicable neighborhood relationships than are dogs. Anchorage is trying to control through the zoning ordinance what should be accomplished under the nuisance animal provisions of the animal control laws.

Most land problems are created by improper utilization of land, such as making changes in contours and drainage patterns to make them fit a projected use rather than fitting the use to the land. The creation of tremendously efficient earth-moving equipment has made it economically feasible to change most land to table-top flatness if the developer so desires.

Major recontouring has far-ranging effects on the entire drainage basin in which it occurs. All neighbors are affected and must react by their own recontouring to adjust to the new drainage patterns. Only the owners of construction equipment profit as an endless drainage problem is created by one unilateral act of one land owner. The State's water laws could have prohibited such actions had they been enforced, but most communities encourage non-enforcement of State laws, and few have local ordinances to control massive recontouring of land or disruption of drainage patterns.

The cost of such disruption of natural land patterns is eventually borne by the taxpayer, as storm sewers, creek channelization, and other drainage systems become necessary. In the same manner, when we allow residential structures in flood plains, we all pick up the cost in the form of increased insurance, disaster funds, and general disruption. Likewise, when we allow intensive development on steep slopes, we increase the costs of operating our communities, as road building and utility installation costs increase. Here again, such development usually has adverse effects on drainage as new erosion occurs.

Many communities have now concluded that it is cheaper to acquire flood plains and steep slopes as public lands than to allow their owners to develop them. In fact, Congress has appropriated open-space funds to acquire such lands on a 75 percent federal/25 percent local basis. Like many federal programs, this one has proved a slender reed upon which to plan since open-space funds are in short supply.

Open space acquisition aids the community whenever portions of land can be utilized for parks and outdoor recreation and for wildlife refuges. Parks and cities do complement each other. Because parks provide necessary open space, it is sometimes desirable to utilize land suitable for development for park space. Parks should be viewed as a utility requirement of any community, the same as water, sewer, or streets. It is a mistake to assume that only large towns and cities need parks. All urban places need them, for they are vital building blocks of community consciousness and spirit. Like schools, they provide places where people can come together.

The importance of parks was recognized by urban planners of the last century. Frederick Olmstead in New York and Chicago,

Dan Burnham in Chicago and Cleveland, Baron Hausmann in Paris — all considered parks and ornamental boulevards as necessary as any other aspect of the city. Until the advent of mass use of the automobile, there were three major factors that shaped the urban landscape of the large cities of America and Europe: the multistory building, the public transit system, and parks. To these must now be added the freeway. Because we gained the automobile and the freeway, many of our newer cities — Los Angeles always being the prime example — have disregarded the other three elements.

But I should not disparage Los Angeles and the style of life it represents. There has to be something good about a city that attracts so many. Los Angeles does have many physical benefits in topography and climate.

A community by its very definition needs common places. It is these common places that are lacking in all but the oldest portions of Los Angeles and most of our newer cities. It is instructive to note that those cities which typify suburban America with its total commitment to individually owned land and individually owned transportation systems are also those places most committed to ultra-conservative political ideologies. William Thompson, in *At the Edge of History,* notes that residents of Orange County seek their recreation at Knotts Berry Farm and Disneyland where they can enjoy re-creations of the New England village with its common land in the center, or enjoy riding a trolley together — even if the trolley is only taking them back to their starting place.

In their lifestyle, these people illustrate the continued dichotomy of man: the social animal and the lonely hunter, the seeker after gaiety and light and the inhabitor of lonely fortresses. It is a question ultimately of which side of man do we wish to encourage in our urban places.

The urban and civilized behavior of the citizens of London's West End can be attributed in large part to St. James, Hyde, and Regent Parks. They are never far from green in the West End. On the other hand, the acerbic disposition of dwellers in east London might be attributed to their lack of parks.

The rich tend to cluster around parks when they are available. Manhattan has its Central Park. It is interesting to speculate what a park would have done for Harlem. Perhaps it is in revenge that Harlem now makes Central Park largely uninhabitable after dark.

The National Urban Council recommends that twenty-five percent of an urban area should be devoted to parks and open spaces. Many of the world's large cities exceed this percentage: London, Berlin, and Zurich are almost 50 percent green. In Hawaii, places that are not even large enough to support a general store have community parks and some are almost as large as the rest of the community. Hawaii has a population density some two hundred times greater than Alaska. Incredibly, it is in Alaska that the complaint is heard, "We cannot afford to give up land for parks and open space."

To turn now to buildings and their relationship to land and community: Doxiadis uses the term *shells* when speaking of buildings and that term can encompass a room or an entire city. Subgroupings include housing, community facilities such as schools and hospitals, shopping centers, and finally, city centers where business and cultural networks merge.

There are two extremes represented in city planning now — Doxiadis, who constantly preaches that all urban planning must relate to man and to the human scale, and Scolari, who sees the city as a vast integrated beehive where man adjusts to the new environment of *arcology,* as the Scolarian hives are termed.

The Greeks never created any open space in their ancient cities over 600 feet in width — the greatest distance at which one person can identify another. In almost all of the world's cities, before the advent of public transit and the automobile, most day-to-day relationships took place within an area one kilometer square, this being the distance that the average adult can walk in fifteen minutes.

Now we use our machine technology to expand our urban mobility. We commute as far as 100 miles to get to work in buildings up to 100 stories. What do we gain from such mobility and such concentration that would not be served equally well by a setting more adjusted to the human scale? Is it surprising that many dwellers of the large cities are seeking other surroundings?

The effect of mobility and concentration is probably felt most acutely by those exposed to the information flow that it generates. A person living in Ketchikan, with its 10,000 inhabitants, may meet in a normal day downtown 200 people of whom only 20 may not be known. This person lives within a system in which information can be absorbed as it comes in. The inhabitant of a major city will encounter that many people on his way to work and know only his immediate neighbors. His information flow network is in a state of constant saturation, and he easily becomes tired and confused.

Another aspect of our buildings that sadly needs attention is their place in maintaining historical continuity and sense of place. It is difficult to isolate that factor in our society which is causing us to create a continent — and ultimately a world — of look-alike buildings, but it is probably because of standardization of materials and techniques. But the inherent drive in Western man towards individuality creates local differentiation where a little architectural homogeneity might be desirable. The net result is that one place looks much like another, and every place is something of a mess.

Visual and noise pollution are ultimate dangers to the future of humanity. We might adjust our intestines to the onslaught of bacteria present in water pollution (as do millions upon millions of Asians), and we might adjust our breathing to the strange atmospheres created by air pollution. But it is doubtful that we can adjust our minds to the noise that assaults us on all sides, and it is doubtful that we can adjust our souls to a continued onslaught of ugliness in our day-to-day landscapes. The adjustment to water and air pollution could possibly be achieved with only minor biological changes, but the adjustment to continued noise and ugliness might change the entire concept of what is human and what humanity ultimately stands for.

What is the factor that makes for a good-looking city as opposed to an ugly one? It is not just having look-alike buildings. Sometimes architectural homogeniety creates breathtaking spectacles as in the Place de la Vendome in Paris or in some of the better streets of brownstone houses in New York. Sometimes it will create utter drabness as in a government housing project in the Soviet Union or the United States.

Sometimes different styles of architecture will go together and simply create an overall pleasing effect. Analyzing some of the world's more renowned boulevards can give us a clue.

The Champs Elysee at first presents a sense of unity and completeness despite the sidewalk cafes and signs that clutter it. Looking at the buildings, one soon discovers that they are all different and only similar in that most are of the same height. Built in the days before elevators were available, most of these structures stopped at eight stories — the maximum stair-climbing plateau for most of the human species.

So one looks for another element that provides continuity, since it seems improbable that buildings of similar size can alone achieve this effect. One finds the other factors in the line of trees on both sides, in the wide sidewalks, and in the anchors at either end — the Arc de Triomphe and the Place de la Concorde. All taken together create that visual masterpiece, the Champs Elysee.

In addition to visual continuity there is historic continuity. If that uniqueness present in every area and community is to be maintained, it must be recognized in architectural forms. This uniqueness does not mean that new forms should not be used or encouraged. It does mean that those forms and styles should have some relationship with climatological and historical realities.

We have some fine buildings in every community in Alaska, but we also have too many that are simply standard imports that represent the least cost per square foot in some other situation and may not even be the cheapest style to use in the rains of the Northwest Coast or the sub-Arctic climate of Anchorage.

Some of the best architecture in the world, especially for homes, has been developed on the Pacific Coast in the past half century. A unique blend of western ranch, Spanish and oriental forms, it is a fluid adaptable style that, in its Pacific Northwest variations, is suited to a rainy temperate climate. In Anchorage and Fairbanks, a regional architecture has not developed since we stopped using round logs. Since I feel most at home in a log house and feel warmest in winter in that style, I still live in one.

Rabindranath Tagore, the Indian philosopher, on his first trip to Europe, remarked about how tenderly the peasants cared for the land in France and Germany compared to India, where the land was simply used and then left to bake and erode when not planted. Primarily, he noted that the European peasant cared about what came after and treated the land as his most valuable possession. Here was a well developed land ethic to sustain European societies.

Aldo Leopold, in *A Sand County Almanac,* stated the principle for a land ethic as follows:

All ethics so far evolved rest upon a single premise: that the individual is a member of a community of interdependent parts. His instincts prompt him to compete for his place in that community, but his ethics prompt him also to cooperate (perhaps in order that there may be a place to compete for). The land ethic simply enlarges the boundaries of the community to include soils, waters, plants, and animals, or collectively: the land.

An ethic, ecologically, is a limitation on freedom of action in the struggle for existence. An ethic, philosophically, is a differentiation of social from anti-social conduct. These are two definitions of one thing. The thing has its origin in the tendency of interdependent individuals or groups to evolve modes of cooperation. The ecologist calls these symbiosis. Politics and economics are advanced symbiosis in which the original free-for-all competition has been replaced, in part, by cooperative mechanisms with an ethical content. We abuse land because we regard it as a commodity belonging to us. When we see land as a community to which we belong, we may begin to use it with love and respect. There is no other way for land to survive the impact of mechanized man, nor for us to reap from it the esthetic harvest it is capable, under science, of contributing to culture. That land is a community is the basic concept of ecology, but that land is to be loved and respected is an extension of ethics.

Perhaps the most serious obstacle impeding the evolution of a land ethic is the fact that our educational and economic system is headed away from, rather than toward, an intense consciousness of land. Your true modern is separated from the land by many middlemen and by innumerable physical gadgets ... To him it is the space between cities on which crops grow. The case for a land ethic would appear helpless but for the minority which is in obvious revolt against these "modern" trends. The "key-log" which must be moved to release the evolutionary process for an ethic is simply this: quit thinking about decent land use as solely an economic problem. Examine each question in terms of what is ethically and esthetically right, as well as what is economically expedient. A thing is right when it tends to preserve the integrity, stability and beauty of the biotic community. It is wrong when it tends otherwise.

I am one of the lucky ones who remembers Alaska's interior when it was all common land. The entire land mass was ours — everyone's — to do with as we pleased. Since there were very few of us and we usually attacked the land with a cruiser axe or a shovel, it was not necessary to think too much about land ethics as we were not harming it much. If we had an ethic it was, "Use the land but don't do anything that will ruin it for the next user." This ethic, of course, applied mainly to the trappers, not to the placer miners who of necessity had to change the face of the land totally. Because they had the big dredges their need of a land ethic was far greater than ours.

Today in Alaska we have forces at work that can totally change the face of the land. What is our land ethic in Alaska, especially in that particular part of Alaska where you reside and have a special responsibility?

THE OPEN-TO-ENTRY LAND EXPERIMENT

Robert A. Durr

THE TALKEETNA Historical Society, a non-profit organization drew up a proposal acceptable to the Alaska Humanities Forum to survey the effects of the land upon the lives of the people in an area including Talkeetna and extending approximately twenty miles north along the tracks and east to Chunilna Creek. Appointed Project Director, I travelled by snowmobile, train, and on foot to tape-record discussions with a high percentage of the settlers on the designated Open-to-Entry lands and with a cross section of "old-timers" and informed individuals in Talkeetna.

The conversations proceeded, informally, along the lines and roughly on the sequence of the following topics:

1. What were your motives in coming to Alaska and life on the land?
2. Have any desirable human values emerged in the course of your experience living in the bush, such as enhanced creativity, learning new skills, and greater awareness of nature?
3. What has been the effect of the land upon human relations, especially as regards the sense of community?
4. What are your ideas about the best use of Alaska's land in terms of optimum population density and the kinds of development, if any, you would consider desirable?
5. What specific recommendations would you make, if any, in modification of the existing public lands policies, especially apropos the Open-to-Entry lands?

This summary of the people's response to these questions will take the topics in sequence. It should be indicated first that the people surveyed probably represent a cross-section of Alaska's population. They ranged in age from 15 to 65, came from all parts of the United States, and from diverse social backgrounds. They thus represent both sides of the generation gap and reflect most of the degrees of differences in values and lifestyle that obtain in Alaska and the United States generally.

1. Motives

In terms of what brought the people to life in the woods, probably the most fundamental motive, shared in varying degrees by virtually everyone consulted, was the desire to get out of the "rat-race" characteristic of the established life-patterns in the States, and to return to the land in hopes of finding there a setting conducive to the creation of a slower, simpler, and healthier life founded upon those values universally recognized as humanistic. None of the settlers on the Open-to-Entry lands whom I talked with were impelled by economic ambitions; none expected or hoped to "make their fortune." While most of the old-timers came to Alaska initially for mainly economic reasons, in accordance with America's preponderant emphasis upon the economic element of life, they soon came to recognize the land itself and the way of life it offered as the real, if underlying reasons why they "fell in love with Alaska" and remained. Subsumed in this basic shared desire to live on the land in its natural state are such individual variations as the wish to "live my own life," to "find myself," to find what is real by simplifying life to its fundamentals, to commune with Nature or contemplate God, to live more creatively or more adventurously, to build a true community, and so forth.

Minnie Swanda came with her husband during the depths of the depression thinking things might be better in a new country. But as she talks about those early days her whole emphasis falls not upon how they did or did not improve their lot economically but upon how they quickly fell in love with the *land*: "You were here because you liked the land . . . You liked the way you were living." She relates how, in fact, after having had to move to Anchorage to make a living (and Anchorage then was more a town than a city), they found Talkeetna, which was a "tiny village," and "just loved it." They got five acres out of town and moved in, despite the harder economic situation: "You get out of a big city because you like the land . . . I still like places where I'm not being pushed, crowded."

Dorothy Jones has lived in Alaska all her life and since 1956 has made Talkeetna her home, where she runs a grocery store. She admitted that she actually wishes the Open-to-Entry program could be closed down: "If I had my 'druthers,' I'd druther see the Open-to-Entry program cut off right at this point, and see 10-20 years from now, what we have." She expressed her fear that "if the land laws continue as they are . . . there won't be a free space left any-where."

2. Creativity

Virtually everyone affirmed that living close to the land in relative isolation from centers of population, convenience, and entertainment has significantly enhanced the creative aspects of life. They found a deep satisfaction in building their own homes whether alone or, as was more frequently the case, with the help of friends and neighbors; in obtaining a large part of their food directly from the land through gardening, foraging, and hunting and fishing, all of which represented the acquisition of skills venerable to mankind but new to many of the settlers; in making their own furniture, rugs, pillows, clothing and so forth, many learning to work with hides or weave baskets, to preserve fish and game, to handle a dog team and the many other skills and kinds of knowledge intrinsic to a more or less self-subsistent life on the land. They all declared, enthusiastically, further, that such activities had profoundly enriched their lives and brought them into closer and more authentic relations with family, friends, neighbors, and — equally important — with nature inself.

Judy Harvey, in explaining how beneficial life in the woods has been for their young son, remarked that "he knows what his father does, which most children never know, and he can relate to that role much better by having his father around more and by seeing what sorts of things he does throughout the day. Sometimes he and Tom go out and cut a tree down, and he rides on the toboggan when Tom brings the wood in. He can see the source where everything comes from and I think that's really beneficial."

3. Interpersonal Relations

Without exception, once again, the people felt that both intra-familial and community relations benefited greatly from the circumstance of their being relatively few people, mostly in small clusters, surrounded by considerable areas of unoccupied and undeveloped land. As regards the quality of interpersonal relations and the possibilities of a genuine community, "bigger" is decidedly *not* "better." The discussions on this score could be encapsulated in the formula that the fewer the people the better their relations. It was common for these settlers to comment that their present experience of cooperation among people and the real sense of community gained through that cooperation and the sharing of a way of life with its attendant values is in sharp contrast with the kind of impersonal and superficial human relations that largely prevails in the crowded urban and suburban centers. And everyone was seriously concerned that the present rapid influx of people would obviate the important life-values they had gained in coming to the woods, that unless the land laws were modified they would shortly find themselves, and the new people as well, living in a rural slum or suburb amidst an ecological wasteland.

When Tom and Ann Mercer's cabin, with everything they owned, including Tom's cash prize for finishing the sled dog race from Anchorage to Nome and the fine sled he had used, burned to the ground one night, leaving them and their two small boys homeless and literally penniless, word spread quickly, and within two or three days they had more cash, clothing, and food than before the fire, and work was begun on a new and better cabin, with people showing up to help from all over the area, including Talkeetna. The days I was there, Tom had at least ten extra men helping on the cabin. It went up fast, despite the mushy spring snow. There were even donations of building supplies and tools and the use of a neighbor's snowmobile. Human relations and community feelings probably reached a plateau during that time. Had there been many more people in the general area it is doubtful that it would have happened, since it appears to be the rule that the greater the number of people, the more superficial their relations. What did happen constitutes a form of wealth unaccountable in the economists' ledgers.

4. Land Use

In accordance with their predominantly humanistic life-values and their positive experiences living year-round in a sparsely populated area, the people surveyed were unanimous in their belief that the primary use of the land, especially and specifically the Open-to-Entry lands, should be for human habitation, with industry and any form of development, including roads, being either forbidden or sharply restricted and regulated. The overwhelming majority believes that clean air and water, a flora and fauna for the most part free of pollutants, and the serene and instructive presence of unadulterated nature, constitute a kind of "public wealth," to borrow former Secretary of the Interior Stewart Udall's phrase, far more essential to human well-being than any economic advantages that might result from the usual types of land use or development as practiced in the "lower 48" and heretofore in Alaska. Further, inasmuch as the improved interpersonal relationships and general sense of community depend upon factors arising from the presence of large tracts of uninhabited and unadorned land, the people feel that any further crowding can only result in the deterioration of the human community as well as of the ecology in general. They believe that, on the whole, the Open-to-Entry area in question has reached or, in many localities, passed the point of optimum population density.

It must be stressed that the settlers' convictions on these points are founded upon their realization of the fact that while the Open-to-Entry Program was set up with the idea of 5 acre *recreational* sites uppermost in mind, the overwhelming majority of people actually living on the land are doing so on a year-round basis in the nature of *homesteading*. This fact alone decisively changes the character and consequences of land use in the OTE areas. Most immediately, for example, it is clear to old-timer and cheechako alike that a family attempting to homestead on only 5 acres with the actuality or likelihood of the surrounding acreage being occupied, cannot attain to any high degree of self-subsistence and must inevitably deplete their wood supply for building and heating purposes within a few years. The consequences to the forest and to the whole ecology, including the human element, would be disastrous.

Tom and Judy Harvey live on a ridge overlooking the Susitna River at about Mile 233 of the Alaska Railroad. There are at present five families living side by side there, with others starting to build. As Tom said, "We do definitely feel the pressure of more people around us, and the threat of still more people moving in — just plot after plot after plot — so that we won't be able to have any real relationships with our neighbors . . . or with the land, because it's hard to relate to everything at once ... Everybody on this ridge talks about getting away, as an escape, a possibility they might do in the near future ... and the reason is because of other people."

Dave Marmor, retired from the Army and living with his family in the woods off Mile 232, fears that the influx of any more entrymen will crowd him out. He thinks that "the people that are here now and that are staked really should have the right to say to the people coming in, 'O.K., fine, that particular area over there is wide open, but right around this area you can't stake. There's enough people here now, and this is all the woods will hold. We're looking ahead five, ten years. It's not that we don't want you. It's just that the land won't hold you.' The time to start doing this is now. Either that or in another five years, *we'll* have to move."

Many, like Sue Roguszka, are concerned that there may not be enough unspoiled land for future generations: "Very frequently I'll sit on the dock and I'll look out and think, you know, there are people in this world who have never had an opportunity to look at the woods, to watch a beaver, or to watch a loon. I really would like to leave part of this for somebody else to come in and enjoy too. Those of us who are on the land have a responsibility to use the land wisely ... so that we can pass on a heritage to our kids and to those who are to come after."

5. Recommendations

The dilemma the OTE lands people face is this: they recognize the right and desirability of the public's having access to the land just as they had, and they do not want to exclude anyone who wishes to share in the real values of living on the land as they have (speculators and developers excepted). At the same time, they are clearly aware that, if the present OTE laws are maintained, allowing the occupancy of adjacent 5 acre tracts blanketing the land, the very values that brought the people to the land and are bringing others would be destroyed.

In wrestling with this dilemma, the people have shaped the following recommendations for changes in the OTE land laws. Insofar as the OTE lands are microcosmic of the land situation in Alaska generally, these recommendations might apply to the overall question of land use.

1) Perhaps the simplest solution deemed desirable by all the entrymen would be to close the present OTE lands to any further occupancy and open new areas to entry, such as the Kuskokwim, Colville, Yukon, Koyukuk, and Delta areas, the Brooks Range, and the north side of the Alaska Range. Several people advised that a closure at this time, before things had gone too far, would permit everyone, including the State, to assess over the next five or ten years what the OTE Program has achieved. As Don Sheldon put it, "If this particular area is saturated, [and] it looks to me that it is, and they intend to hold the line on the Open-to-Entry sites, I say close the local areas that are saturated and open some of the areas that are not saturated."

Gene Roguszka concurs with the general principle and suggests that "when the filings reach the one-third stage of land within a section, a moratorium be placed on further filings. The moratorium should last for a period of 36 months, the idea being this: give the opportunity for things in that particular area to stabilize." He adds that a provision would be necessary to prevent the unstaked areas from being used in the interim so that they would still be desirable if and when the Program were reopened in those areas.

2) The second most prevalent proposal was to increase the acreage to each entryman. The specific numbers suggested ranged from 10 acres per person (a man and wife could then claim 20 acres between them) to 40 acres per family unit. (Surprisingly, perhaps, no one seriously urged the adoption of the homestead-scale of 160 acres, because they did not feel that much land to be necessary to subsistence and the best interests of the ecology and because they are aware of the abuses and speculation that have plagued the Homestead Act.) The greater acreage allotment would be retroactive in that entrymen who have already filed on 5 acres could expand their present site to the maximum acreage allowed. In cases where 5 acre plots have been leased or bought adjacent to one another, as is frequently the case around lakes, the entrymen would have perforce to expand to the rear of his original 5 acres in "railroad car" fashion. This would at least be preferable to being restricted within the original allotment. It would have to be specified that the additional acreage be contiguous with the present site, in order to obviate the temptation to speculate.

77

Jim and Gloria Burbeau of Talkeetna felt strongly that if a man or family can "prove up" by making a go of it on the land, the State should survey and give them the land. There is widespread disgruntlement over the State's "being in the real estate business": in effect, managing the people's inheritance in order to sell it to them. The taxation of the land consequent to a person's receiving title to it is all the revenue the State should require, it is argued.

3) Two other closely related proposals were:

a) To withdraw "green-belt" areas from occupancy around those localities which, because of desirability, have become densely populated, such as around most lakes and streams. This proposal would leave the "green-belt" acreage in the State's hands and open to the public for hiking, camping, and so forth, but it would permit the entrymen within its enclosure to utilize the resources, such as timber and firewood. The optimum extent of the "green-belt" that would afford a sustained yield of wood, berries, wild-life, and so forth, as well as guarantee an expanse of unoccupied land adequate to the psychological and spiritual needs of the people, can probably be best determined in consultation with forestry experts. But the people's initial estimate is that the "green-belt" would have to be no less than 60 acres deep on the score of the latter consideration alone.

b) A proposal to "checkerboard" the 5 acre plots was made by a couple from Anchorage who use their 5 acre site for recreational purposes. The idea is to prevent the possibility of the 5 acre sites being located immediately adjacent to one another, and thereby insuring a greater degree of privacy, quiet, and unspoiled landscape. This plan is obviously most feasible for the recreational use of the land and would be inadequate to the needs of the year 'round homesteader. A combination of a "checkerboard" and "green-belt" patterning of certain areas might be better than either alone.

4) A large proportion of the people living on the land expressed concern, anger, and resentment over the prevalence of speculation. With land for human use so much at a premium, they vigorously object to those who would "tie it up" just to make money from it. In their opinion, it should not be possible for anyone simply to

spend a few hours on the land, pay fees, and eventually obtain title. They feel, therefore, that the land laws should contain some provision that would preclude speculation and favor those entrymen who wish to sustain themselves on the land, that there should be some requirement that an individual actually live on the land at least part of the year.

Mike Fisher sums it up: "I'd like to see some aspect of the law that tended to preclude speculation with Open-to-Entry lands . . . The law should have some provision in it that favors an individual who will go out and sustain himself on the land. And by sustain himself . . . I mean actually go out there and live on the land, and learn some things, and make some observations . . . I think that a requirement to obtaining eventual title to this land should be at least a token amount of living on it. I don't believe it should be possible to just go out and set foot on the land once . . . and wind up with that land. It's that sort of thing that encourages useless and blind and deleterious speculation."

The people are not adamant about these recommendations as constituting the only solutions to their dilemma. They mainly wish to make their problem clear to those who represent them and are empowered to take whatever action would effect a solution in the best interests of the land and the people, preserving those essential life-values that the humanistic use of the land cultivates.

THE NEED FOR WILDERNESS
Margaret E. Murie

I GREW UP in Fairbanks. Two months after graduation from the University of Alaska, I married a government biologist and spent the following years with him in the field in all his studies. On expeditions in Alaska, Wyoming, and New Zealand we had three children along with us. In later years, when my husband was Director of the Wilderness Society, we had more expeditions, more travels, more work for the preservation of wilderness.

Now I have come back to my home country after an eight-year absence. My own bird's eye view (which may be altered in the weeks following up here this summer) is that Alaska is both physically and emotionally split by the Pipeline. But I don't want or intend to talk about the Pipeline. I'm sure Alyeska is building it swiftly, expeditiously, and with environmental concern. But what the Pipeline started, Alaska will have to deal with in 1990 with oil, fish, minerals, timber, recreation, and people competing for them. Perhaps, we may learn a bit about humanities — human, man — and whether man is human enough or deserves that term. And I hope very much that we shall have here at this forum not only words, but some definite suggestions for action.

For myself I should like to enter here a plea for the consideration of the non-humanities, non-human values, for the land itself, but also for man — part of man's need. I grew up in Fairbanks when James Wickersham was battling in Congress for a government railroad for Alaska. Wood was the only fuel. Hillsides were stripped of birch forest to feed the boilers at all the little placer mines. Every household burned ten cords of wood a winter. The water-man brought you two or four buckets of water each day. The nameless hero came in the night to remove the necessary from the privy in the woodshed. Nothing was easy, but everyone counted. Everyone was cared for — a bigger and beautiful library, and hospitals. There were dress up parties, home-grown concerts, and plays, and always dances. I don't think people dance enough any more. Dance all night. Go to the Model Cafe for breakfast. Go home. Change your clothes and go to work. There were quarrels, but always humor. And, we had the march scandal too. It was expected always

— at least one. As a small child, I remember the whistles and the siren blowing and everyone rushing to First Avenue — an impromptu parade. Dear old Mr. Gobracht's German Band was marching and someone had found a coal scuttle and was waving it as he marched. Wickersham had won. Alaska was going to have a railroad. The coal mines could be opened. It was coal then. Now it is oil. But what a different accompaniment! Then the placer days were over and the great slump came during World War I. The railroad was not finished until 1922. Then came the second gold boom. This time it was the big companies from outside. And big dredges. Now, that boom is over. Now, it is oil. Joe Meeker in his *Comedy of Survival* says, speaking of a pioneering species in any environment, "These are highly generalized, flexible and adaptable creatures, capable of surviving despite the inhospitable nature of their environment. Pioneers must be aggressive, competitive and tough." The early Alaskans were all these things. For surely Alaska resisted rape with everything she had. Biting cold, rampaging streams, heartbreaking muskeg swamps, formidable mountains, stormy seas, impenetrable forest, *and mosquitos!* Now man is above all that — he flies. No place is too remote. No place is safe from man's touch. Joe Meeker also says, "with the machine empowered the garden is doomed." Man was little in those days. Now he is big with his bulldozer. But let's think for a moment about the Chief of Police of Fairbanks being interviewed in his office recently. He was calm and relaxed. He said, "Oh, it's just another boom. After a while it will go away."

This past winter I spent many hours reading the journals my husband has kept during all the years he worked in Alaska as a naturalist. And I should like to quote here from his journal written at Nenana, Alaska, September 5, 1925. You may remember, some of you, that Nenana was a boom town during the building of the railroad, and especially because of the great bridge they built across the Tanana there. The notes say: "I think of the old stampede days when steamers plied frantically up and down the Yukon, when hammer and saw made joyful sound of industry, and hope and enthusiasm filled the air. And now, these empty buildings, broken windows, and silence. I look out of my hotel window. The hill across the Tanana glows with gold and yellow and pale green of the birches. The red of the blueberry bushes in Autumn dress penetrating the dark spruce. It's pleasing, giving me a wholesome feeling. The old gold rush is gone — must always go. But this golden hill has always been there — it's still there. And autumn among the birches belongs to a stable civilization with homes and children, schools and swimming holes. Slower growth but more desirable for Alaska."

Will it "go away"? Or, are we already locked into a system which is voracious? Locked into opposing camps? Will we be so blind and helpless that we lose the most precious things, after all?

I quote here from an article by Jim Hunter: "So those facing North to the wilderness have two radically different visions on what to do with it. There are many who subscribe to development and growth as synonymous with national security and greatness; there are many others who view the preservation of Alaska as a turning point, as a welcome antivenin for an already poisoned earth. Perhaps the real enemy of the wilderness is an invalid American dream. Perhaps too late we're learning that a diet of metal and oil will kill us. Perhaps too late we will discover that the valid new frontiers exist in the spirit and in technology and that no matter where the new frontiers will be, human beings cannot do without wilderness. Alaska, the accidental purchase, has left this nation, with a storehouse of green wilderness-vitamin A-1.

"While irresponsible developers, and this does not mean all developers, push to get there first, to get rich first, they fail to realize the greatest resource Alaska has to offer a sick America is clean air and pure water and wild lands. And it is not just the developers. Because without a population which applauded them and purchased their products, they could not continue. The developer may be the hammerhead, but society is the handle and all the power coming down behind it. And as sure as society can smash the hammer down on Alaskan Wilderness, it can also throw the hammer away. And this time around will be the last time."

I don't need to tell you that much has happened in Alaska since I was up here in 1967. That summer I saw parts of Alaska I had never seen before because I was travelling with my friend, Mildred Capion, who was making a film, "Alaskan Summer". On our return that autumn, I spoke at a banquet in Seattle and I'm going to tell you a few of the things I said then, which was eight years ago now.

"I went back to Alaska this summer, travelled 10,000 miles with my friend in her Ford Travel Wagon. Ferried to Prince Rupert and Wrangell and it rained, to Petersburg and it rained, and to Juneau and it was lovely. Flew to Fairbanks for commencement at the University of Alaska, and back to Juneau and Glacier Bay for 5 great days; to Sitka and it was beautiful; and back on the ferry to Haines and 4 wonderful days, and on to the Interior to Anchorage and Homer; by ferry to Kodiak for 6 days, then to Kenai and the Moose Range and a canoe trip and a flight over the Kenai Mountains and to Palmer and the dairy farms; McKinley Park, and to Fairbanks and the Steese Highway to Circle, and to Valdez and by ferry to Cordova and the salmon canneries. Back over the highway to Tok and the Taylor Highway to Eagle on the Yukon and then to Dawson and Whitehorse and Carcross and the railroad to Skagway and return. And finally all the way home to Moose, Wyoming. We were not long on the ferry out of Prince Rupert before getting the feel of the new Alaska. There was a fascinating mixture of people on board. Going through Wrangell Narrows at dusk, very quiet, under a slow bell, everyone watching those close shores. A young man, a pile-driver operator in the timber industry, was talking quietly. He said, 'Never a dull moment in the new State of Alaska. If you keep your eyes and ears open for what's around you — and we don't have so much artificial amusements up here, so we keep our eyes and ears open for what's around us.' The new Alaskans. The young men all love the life. Some of the wives do, some don't. The young mechanic who towed us into Tok for repairs said that he loved hunting in the fall and snowshoeing in the winter, but his wife hates it. In Fairbanks a taxi driver told my friend, 'I came up here 12 years ago for two weeks. Never been back, no desire to go back.' At a cannery near Haines, a young fisherman was mending his nets, 'I wouldn't live anywhere else. Always something beautiful to look at. Wake up in the morning, look out the window, always something beautiful — nice to look at.' Why do they love it? The land itself most of all, I think. Even though some of them are busy altering it, busy killing the thing they love, making it like all the other states. But most of Alaska's new people do love it. Will there be enough who care? The struggle will be between these two —

both new. One group thinking of a whole life, the other making money and getting out. As for the old timers, the Sourdoughs, they live in nostalgia and can they be blamed? There were, in spite of hardships, so many charming things in that old life — dog teams, stern-wheel steamers on the rivers, absolute freedom. If a prospector didn't make it in one creek there were plenty of other creeks to try. At Forty-Mile last summer we stopped to take movies at the road house where they were raising Siberian Huskies. One of the partners said, 'So where's there to go anymore? Up at Barrow they say there's only two dog teams left. Everybody's got those skidooes, and natural gas piped into their houses. So where's there to go anymore? Forty-Mile's the only place left, I guess. The people there don't *want* that new stuff.'

"What did my friend film? Glacier Bay, a threat of mining; Sitka, the pulp mill, a big freighter loading just as we pulled into the cove; at Haines another huge freighter loading logs, 4,500,000 board feet at a load. At Kodiak diversified fishing has arrived there. A huge new fish plant is being built. At Kenai, oil rigs in the forest and offshore. Much of this industry must be accepted. But, the overriding thought in my mind is, while all this is going on, what is being left for the one industry which can be most lucrative, non-destructive, self-perpetuating for all times, a commodity in short supply in other world markets? The industry of simply letting people come to see and enjoy Alaska. What is next for Alaska? What will be left of the distinctive Alaskan features which draw the tourist? We talked to many tourists this past summer, and what were they looking for? Size, vastness, magnificence, naturalness, informality of life, enthusiasm, happy people, and mountains and glaciers, waterfalls, great trees, whales, porpoises, birds, all the other wildlife, but also, a glimpse of the old Alaska and of the everyday life of its people. I saw tourists stopping at a garden in Fairbanks admiring the cabbages, the peas, and all the rest, and talking to the white-haired old-timer who was working in the garden. At Miller House on the Steese Highway we stopped in to see if they served breakfast. The old proprietor said: 'No, we don't do, that anymore but come on in and set awhile and light your pipe and visit anyway.' These are the things tourists will remember and take home with them. The life, the feelings of those who live in Alaska.

There are some who want a martini and a thick steak every night. That is one kind of tourist. But there are others, and I think they'll be more numerous, who are seeking, I believe, a picture of the past. They liked that Alaska 67 Exposition, not just because it was a picture of the past, but because that past had a virility, a ruggedness, an individual freedom that is fast disappearing, and for which they have a longing in the midst of our copy-cat, plastic civilization.

"Alaska has lots of problems. But I am hopeful she will solve some. And in my mind, the most important thing is saving the land itself. And the problems here are big business and big government. What is all the business for? Millions for a few?

"Again, here we have the new people and the old who want money, and the people who seek a whole life who feel what kind of life and future without the great big beautiful land itself, plus, the Sourdoughs that are appalled at the whole thing. I hope there will be an Alaska for the young mechanic at Tok, for the young student who wants to explore glaciers, for the Indian or Eskimo who still wants to live in his village, for the young University couple who merely want to live in a little house in the woods, and for the young fisherman who wants to keep on fishing in his own little boat and look out every morning at something nice."

Well, eight years have gone by since I said all those words in Seattle.

What now? What are the forces working in Alaska? Big business, big labor, big government, state and federal bureaucrats held upright by pressure from all sides, and getting the slings and arrows from all sides; scientists, government and otherwise, who carry on their beloved research and wonder if anybody will listen to them; wonder if the forces will listen to them. Old Alaskans who are on the band-wagon of all the new business, old Alaskans who wish they had never heard the word *pipeline* and wonder whether to go somewhere else; new Alaskans who want a good simple life, and are willing to work in the battle to save something of the real Alaska; and, perhaps most important of all, the Natives who are also divided between those who want to keep their own ways, their own village life, and those who want the Natives to be right in there with development, and dollars, and the "good things of life."

What *are* the good things of life? And can all these forces (none of which are just going to "go away") realize that they must talk, think, act, eat together? Who is right? No one completely, of course. But given all these forces, what philosophy will be followed for a lifestyle in 1990? How much of Alaska for change, for development, for profits, for jobs, for more population? How much for the land itself as it now is? With all its potential gifts of subsistence living, of scientific discoveries, of helpful recreation, of inspiration. On this point do we have to split and declare war? I plead for a plan under which there will always be room for a healthy economy, for a healthy population, with a great deal of Alaska left alone.

In Wyoming, I live on a former private in-holding in Grand Teton National Park, on the Snake River bottoms, in the woods at 6,-400 feet altitude. Our place used to be a dude ranch and there are three houses on it. The wildlife is plentiful. I had a moose come along the road and say goodbye to me as I was leaving for the airport the other morning, and we're all zealous to keep it that way. I counted 18 species of mammals on that 77 acres. Last fall a cat appeared, probably dropped off by some tourist going by. I called the Rangers. They came with live traps and lots of good fishy bait and the cat defeated all of us — and our efforts. And, somehow, that creature managed to survive our winter — six feet of snow on the level, blizzards, cold. In April, the snow still deep, the woman who lives in the middle house on the ranch came into her kitchen one evening at dusk, and there saw two dark blobs on the bird tray which is attached to the kitchen window. A mother porcupine and her baby had been around all winter and that was normal to see them there. But there was a third blob — yes, the cat! Up there on the bird tray eating with the porcupines! You wonder why I'm telling you this. Well, it occurred to me, if cats and porcupines can eat together and tolerate each other, shouldn't conservationists and businessmen be able to do likewise? And, not only these two forces, but all the others?

I think we have not had the courage to be entirely frank with one another, and this is a point in history when we must be. And, we must talk together. I think my main theme is this, That perhaps man is going to be overwhelmed with his own cleverness. That he may even destroy himself with this same cleverness. And, I firmly believe that one of the very few hopes for man is the preservation of the wilderness we now have left and the greatest reservoir of that medicine for man lies here in Alaska. This sounds radical, I know. I don't mean to be saying that all the modern inventions and discoveries and developments are bad for man. I remember the old days and I know they weren't *always* the "good old days." What I'm trying to say is that somewhere along the line we have lost control of the things we have created. We have learned to need all the comforts and refinements and things and gadgets which all the technology has presented to us. We are constantly being bombarded with beguiling messages about how much we need all these things. And, big corporations, big bureaucracies feed on themselves, become such entities in themselves, so imbued with the great American dream that growth is a God and that bigger is better and that the thought of decreasing size or a steady State society is an anathema, that to me they have become terrifying. So I'm beginning to wonder where in all this complexity of things is there going to be a voice which says, "Look, where are we going? Hadn't we better stop and look ourselves over?" Perhaps the voices will come from many directions — from the Native villages, from the smaller communities, from the bureaucrats, from the legislators — who knows?

I recommend to your notice the articles by Doug McConnell and Stephen Reeve and by Larry Mayo in the Fall, 1974, issue of the *Alaska Conservation Review.* There are specific suggestions here for input from the public by use of the media into plans for the future of Alaska. I recommend Sam Wright's suggestions in his recent newsletter from Tasseraluk Institute that there be a state-wide education program on what Alaskans want for the future based on grassroots meetings, media presentation, and questionnaires. Does that sound too complicated?

To put it simply, we must all get into the act. If there were only some potent inspiration which would cause every Alaskan to sit down and write in a few words what he wants for his State for the future and send it in to some central clearing house, that would be an example of democracy in action, wouldn't it? And a storehouse of information for decision. If I were required to write such a page, I would first give homage to those Alaskans who are already leading a simple life with a minimum of things, self-sustaining, on renewable resources. And I would say, "For goodness sake, let them have control of their land and the chance to show the rest of us how it is done." We can agree that there is no turning the clock back. The people are here. The economy must remain. But, with some foresight, some scrutinizing of man's real needs, we could begin to have a plan for Alaska and it would begin with each town and each borough.

But underlying all the meetings and the talks and the plans it seems to me is the great doom-thought: when all of Alaska's non-renewable resources are dug out, piped away, cut down — what lifestyle then? And here I submit once more my theme that man, too clever, too far away from the earth, is not happy. I believe that man needs wilderness for five reasons: (1) wilderness preservation for space — elbow room for man — untouched by man; (2) for scientific research. For man's benefit, of course, but also for that of all other creatures — plant and animal. We so far know just enough to know that we haven't begun to know all. That there are all kinds of things to be discovered in the natural world which cannot be discovered anywhere else; (3) for water-shed protection. To keep man's busy, selfish world healthy; (4) for physical recreation of all kinds to keep man's selfish to unselfish body healthy; and (5) for what it gives man's spirit.

There is something elemental and unchangeable here I think. Perhaps there are men who feel no need for nature. They are fortunate in a way perhaps. But for those who somehow feel unnurtured, missing something, groping for something satisfying, surely there should still be a place, a big place — wilderness. Again, man for all his ego is not the only creation. Other species have some rights too. Wilderness itself, the basis of all our life, does it have a right to live on? Having furnished all the requisites of our proud materialistic civilization, our neon-lit society, does it have a right to live on? Do we have enough reverence for life to concede to wilderness this right? I submit that when all the non-renewable resources are gone, Alaska could still have a resource which will support a healthy economy, and a happy life for her people for all time. And that this happy possibility for lifestyle 1990 depends on how much of unspoiled Alaska is saved now. I know it is very poor taste to quote from one's own books, but somehow I could not find any other way to say what I wanted to say at the end of this talk. So I do quote from the preface to *Two in the Far North*, which was published in 1962: "What, after all, are the most precious things in a life? We had a honeymoon in an age when the world was sweet and untrammelled and safe. Up there in the Koyukuk there were very few machines of any kind; but there was joy in companionship and in the simple things — like the crackle of a fire, having tea and bread while the rain pattered on the roof, a chance meeting with a friend on the dog-team trail ... Here in Alaska people still count, as much today as in the twenties. I would love to think the world will survive its obsession with machines to see a day when people respect one another all over the world. It seems as clear as a shaft of the Aurora that this is our only hope. My prayer is that Alaska will not lose the heart-nourishing friendliness of her youth — that her people will always care for one another, her towns remain friendly and not completely ruled by the dollar — and that her great wild places will remain great and wild and free, where wolf and caribou, wolverine and grizzly bear, and all the Arctic blossoms may live on in the delicate balance which supported them long before impetuous man appeared in the North. This is the great gift Alaska can give to the harassed world."

ALASKA'S INDIGENOUS LIFESTYLE
Joseph W. Meeker

LET'S pause to consider who we are and what kinds of things we do to ourselves. Our institutions are crumbling, especially our universities, and along with them may go the intellectual way of life that universities represent, where words often substitute for things and where information takes the place of wisdom. Page Smith, when he retired from the University of California, spoke sharply and clearly about inadequacies within that educational system, and his remarks apply to many other systems as well. William Irwin Thompson also left universities for another kind of life. Monroe Price told us of his experiments outside law schools, and of his discovery of the big differences between being a lawyer rather than a professor of law. And I am busy working at a new university that is in some ways dedicated to the obsolescence of all universities. And yet all of us, as you probably have noticed, continue to speak the university's language and to organize our experience by its conceptual methods — abstraction, logic, rational discourse, historical analysis. Just to relieve my own mind, and maybe yours as well, I'd like to avoid these methods for a few moments.

The feelings and the understanding I acquired from living in the Alaskan environment for ten years didn't consist of concepts or of ideas. And I find that they don't translate very easily into words or into lectures. Instead, I find, reflecting honestly on them, that the significant things that happened to me in that period were people and animals and things and actions and events. Those, I think, are the ingredients of an Alaskan lifestyle.

Rather than defining a lifestyle by the ideologies and concepts that go into it, I wonder if it is possible to define it by the people and the things they do in their environment. Let me try to recall the people who, in my mind, represented what seemed to me distinctively and peculiarly Alaskan, and try to isolate some of the qualities in their lives and some of the events that we had shared together that helped to create the impression that they were genuine Alaskans. Most of them will be people that you don't know or haven't heard of, but the events may strike you as typical of experiences that you have had in Alaska as well.

There's a fellow living near McKinley Park at Deneki Lakes named Bill Nancarrow. A small community has grown up around Bill, and he has nourished it with his hands for the past twenty-five or thirty years. When I met Bill in 1957, I was a park ranger in my early twenties. My wife Marlene and I were newlyweds. Ginny Nancarrow, Bill's wife, took Marlene under her wing and taught her how to live in the bush, as Bill taught me. Marlene learned a reverence for the food which came only once a month and sometimes not then. She learned to avoid waste and to prepare a recipe when every ingredient had to be substituted. From Bill I learned about logs and dogs and sleds, and about the joys of working like a craftsman even when no one was there to admire the work. Bill and Ginny were experts at many crafts, and all of their activities were united around the land they lived on. They were whole people, able to be happy alone but ready to share their lives with others. From them we learned much about how to cope with a difficult environment, and with ourselves.

Ginny spent most of her time doing housewifely things around the cabin — cooking, cleaning, and taking care of the daily chores of household existence. She took great pleasure in her life. She also liked to help Bill peel logs for the cabins he was building, and she knew why she did it. Housework was too temporary and transient to suit her. She would always have to wash that dish again, clean that floor again: most of her life was like that. But when she peeled a log, she knew she would never have to peel *that* log again. Ginny wanted to participate in something that would endure as part of the land she loved.

Ginny contracted cancer and was sent to a hospital in Seattle for treatment. Her case was terminal and she was put in a nursing home there to await death. But it wasn't long before she decided to leave, contrary to her doctor's orders, contrary to all the advice she received, and with grim warnings of the pain she would face, and she returned to Deneki Lakes, where there was no medical help. She had decided to live her final days, and they turned out to be months, on the land that had defined her life. One day, after lunch when the dishes had been done, she went upstairs to her bed and was dead two hours later. Ginny knew a lot about suffering, and she knew how important it was to suffer quietly.

Bill Nancarrow could afford only a short time for grief before he went out to the shop and started constructing a coffin for Ginny. He built a tight box, well seamed and jointed; it was a sturdy, solid, hand-done, well-made coffin created with love. A few friends came over at Bill's request, and said a few words together over Ginny's body before Bill put the coffin on a skid behind his little bulldozer and drove off across the tundra to a burial place that he and Ginny had selected. No one else went along. There are not many places in the world where a death in the family can have that kind of simplicity and dignity.

There was another fellow at McKinley Park at that time, and many people have seen what he does. Charlie Ott is a wildlife photographer. He wasn't always. He was once a hunter and trapper, but the wild animals of Alaska converted him into a dedicated conservationist. He saw animals here in a way that he had never seen them before. Charlie has worked for the last twenty-five years or so and is now retired, as a garbage man and general handyman at McKinley Park. Why? So he could be where the animals were. Charlie hauled garbage for the Park Service, and he photographed animals. You'll find his work in *Audubon Magazine, The National Geographic,* and on practically every calendar that has been printed about Alaska. Charlie also hates those things that threaten what he loves. I've seen him stand on the tundra and scream at airplanes that were flying near a herd of caribou and throw rocks into the air, knowing he couldn't hit them, but knowing also that he had to express how he felt.

People around McKinley Park also know Ginny Wood and Celia Hunter. They founded Camp Denali near Kantishna. They spent some twenty years scratching that place out of a rocky hillside in a very unlikely spot beyond Wonder Lake ninety miles out on the Park road. They battled the roads and the supplies and the Park Service for years, not to mention mosquitos and miners and tourists. Solving impossible problems became a way of life for them, and it was a dull day that included no disasters.

Alaskan business people are different, too. Lou and Madeline Noreen ran the food service which sent us those groceries every month. They saw their business as a service to people who needed it. They were the Anchorage friends for many people who lived in the bush, always ready to help in any way they could. Their business was a circle of friendships more than a source of wealth.

There are well-known people, too, like the Murie family. In the thirties Adolf Murie lived with the wolves of Mt. McKinley and learned about wolves what nobody before then had ever known. Olaus and Marty Murie loved the Brooks Range and almost single-handedly established the Arctic Wildlife Range there. Marty is still writing books about Alaska. Everyone's heard of Don Sheldon, a crazy bush pilot, but shrewd enough to survive and die of more-or-less natural causes after a career in one of the world's most dangerous professions. The most interesting student I ever had was Eric Forrer, from the Yukon Delta, who came into my freshman class at the University of Alaska. It was the first time in his life he had ever been in a classroom of any kind, and he knew nothing of classroom etiquette. On his first day in class he strode up to the front of the room, started writing on the blackboards and lecturing to the students. I was in his way, so I sat down and he took over the class. He had never learned the student habit of sitting numbly through classes, or of giving to professors the responsibility of his education.

Well, that's my small list. Anybody who has lived in Alaska very long could add dozens of names with more bizarre and more revealing episodes than any I've mentioned. None of these people write earth-shaking books, none of them formulate great ideas, but I think their philosophies are profound, and I think there is wisdom in those people. They express their wisdom in their actions. All of them could, and probably should, have books written about them, but most readers without an experience of Alaska would never understand the books.

When Alaskans write books, they usually produce bad ones. When they produce concepts they usually produce faulty ones. But serious and important actions are well produced here. Maybe this is a non-verbal or at least an unwritten world, where art and thought find direct means of expression rather than indirect means through symbols. Maybe Alaska isn't a place for words, but for sensations and feelings and thoughts that come together around the land, the people, and the animals who live together here. Alaskans express themselves best by responding actively and directly to the land.

Alaska is not the place for tragic heroes. It will probably never produce a saint. There may never be a great Alaskan philosopher to give the world some new system of thought. All pretentions aside, Alaskans are comic characters. Like comic heroes in literature, they devote themselves to coping with adversity, struggling to retain some kind of equilibrium in their lives, trying to survive as best they can. They offer an example to the world, I think, of what people are capable of doing in hard times and in very hard places. That knowledge may be more important than any philosophy for the future of humanity.

The real point to Alaska does not lie in taming the wilderness or advancing the frontiers of civilization or conquering nature. As the poet Dante said, the purpose of climbing a mountain is not to conquer the mountain, but to conquer oneself. That's what an Alaskan lifestyle is all about: conquering oneself. It takes all the wit, skill, and imagination that humans are capable of, and it is a high human function rooted deeply in our species. A French thinker, Montaigne, at the end of his very full life, concluded that the highest possible achievement of mankind was merely "to live appropriately." That is what Alaskans do best when they are attentive to their land, and to one another. Appropriate living is more important here than finding the right words for the right ideas.

There was a Greek named Plato, a couple of thousand years ago, who made a point that great art and great philosophy should be leisure activities pursued by people who are freed of the daily business of grubbing for a living. In Plato's view somebody at the lower end of the social scale, or, in a modern version, some machine, is supposed to produce surpluses so that people like musicians and philosopher kings can be free to contemplate goodness and truth and beauty. Wherever that idea has been accepted a great gap has opened up between people who live by their actions and people who live by their thoughts.

Plato's logic came to Alaska, I think, with the first white settlers. Since then it has often been assumed that the proper Alaskan lifestyle is a life of action which excludes the arts, the humanities, and significant thought. After all, who needs poetry, music, and painting in a tough place like this? Hunting for animals or gold or oil on mountaintops is assumed to be incompatible with hunting for illusive ideas or beauty. Alaskans, we hear over and over again, are doers. Thinkers ought to live farther south where life is much more comfortable.

Plato's idea, which is the basis for the formation of a working class, and for much of the industrial civilization we've inherited, makes very little sense when it is applied to indigenous Alaskan lifestyles. Among Alaskan Natives, for instance, the skills of hunting are simply not separable from those of dancing or carving or religious life. The same is true for most white people who have lived on an intimate basis with the Alaskan natural environment. Alaskans don't need to buy leisure at the expense of some working class. In Alaska leisure is a free gift bestowed upon all by the Alaskan .winter. I have never had more time for reflection and I have never enjoyed beauty more than during those long cold winters spent in McKinley Park. At 50° below zero there are plenty of things to do, including creative art, serious thought, and significant human relationships. Winter, for anybody who lets himself really experience it, has a way of turning us first inward upon ourselves, and then outward towards others.

For many people who come here from the southern centers of civilization, the first Alaskan winter is often a terror of self-analysis. Darkness and cold combine to create a sense of confinement — literally to one's house or one's workcamp, and figuratively, to one's own inner feelings or one's soul. Anybody who has never before thought about having a soul is likely then to experience a tough time. The high suicide and divorce rates of February, the need then for psychoanalysis, attest to the failures of soul that accompany every Alaskan winter. Anyone who can't live with his own inner life is unlikely to live very well in Alaska's winter environment. The winter exploration of oneself, if it's successful, makes it possible to accept and to affirm the existence of others. The dark night of the soul that is described by saints and by poets leads at its best to a recognition of mankind, and a compassion for other people and other creatures. In the same way I think the darkness of an Arctic winter creates warmth and closeness among those who experience it together. Mid-winter gatherings and parties have become art forms in themselves in interior Alaska, and they've always been that among the Eskimos and Indians. So, too, is the tradition of helping others, whether it be to raise a cabin wall, attend a sick dog, or to start a cold car. Friendliness is very serious business in the North, for it expresses the affirmation of oneself through the affirmation of others. It is a philosophical principle expressed through actions more than through words. In Alaska, it arises through the normal thoughts and actions of people as they respond together to the conditions of winter.

As more and more industrial technology has been introduced to the North, it has become increasingly possible to pretend that winter doesn't exist at all. Oil companies have managed to bring some Southern water north with them in the form of heated swimming pools at places like Prudhoe Bay. They have established controlled environments where the temperature never drops below plus 65° F. all winter long, and living quarters where darkness is never allowed to become oppressive. The idea, of course, is to permit the lifestyle of Houston north of the Arctic Circle. All you have to do in order to enjoy that fantasy is to lie to yourself, and many people are very good at it. Such people don't have to trouble about discovering themselves or others or even the land that they're living on. They neither learn from, nor do they contribute to, an Alaskan way of life. In fact, we could ignore them altogether if their presence didn't threaten other ways of life that are genuinely adapted to this land.

Very few people come to Alaska by accident. Most have a purpose of some kind for being here. It isn't easy to get here, and it isn't easy to stay. Strong values and beliefs are necessary simply to justify one's presence in this part of the world. Virtually everybody in Alaska believes in something. That in itself is enough to distinguish Alaskans from people who live in easy places like Italy or Southern California where it's possible to drift in by accident and live your entire life without ever wondering why you're there. Anybody lacking a powerful reason for being in Alaska had better leave as quickly as possible to search for some other place where reasons are not required. Here they are required. The values and the reasons that motivate people to live in Alaska can be lumped into two general categories: those derived from somewhere else, and those that are indigenous to the Alaskan land itself.

The "somewhere else" values come generally from the traditions of warm and temperate cultures. Wealth and power are very high on that list of values and they're sufficient to motivate many of the boomers and the rip-off types who come North. Others believe in the myth of the frontier, which has been around since ancient Greek times, to spur people toward taming wild land and bringing it under human control. These are the people who dream of farming the tundra like prairie sodbusters, who want to exterminate the predators like Daniel Boone, and the people who want to carve great cities out of the wilderness. There are still others who come here in reaction *against* the values of other places. People who are fed up with cities and wars and civilized mayhem often seek escape by an imagined return to nature, which Alaska is supposed to provide. The trouble is that they are dreams, which always remain connected to some other place, as if one were living in Alaska only to prove something to people in Chicago or Los Angeles. The people who live by such values can spend many years here without ever really noticing what Alaska is all about, because their hearts are elsewhere.

Many people, however, are not here to take something away, or to get away from some other place, but come here because they love what Alaska *is*. These are the people who enjoy large spaces in which there is nothing human, who appreciate wild animals because of their wildness, who love the solitude and the spectacle of winter and who want to feel it within themselves, rather than simply observing it through thermopane glass. They enjoy the experience of extremes, like the darkness of winter or the endless sunlight of summer, and the hundred degree difference between indoor and outdoor temperatures. They accept and enjoy the fact that they live in a hard place and they change themselves in order to meet its conditions. They remake themselves to suit the land; they don't expect to remake the land to human measures. When they find one another they enjoy companionship. But finding other people is usually not their main goal. Other people, like the otherness of nature, remain essentially *other*. That is, the things that are outside oneself, human and non-human, are assumed to have an integrity of their own which must be recognized and respected. From that point of view it is not necessary, nor is it desirable, to take possession of everything, or to value only those things that bring personal satisfaction. Alien and even dangerous things have a right to exist according to their own rules, just as pleasant things do.

Such values have not often been taught by the cultural traditions of temperate places, and yet they are implicit in the Alaskan lifestyle. They are the values that arise indigenously in many of the world's hard places, wherever they may be. Alaskans who have learned to live well on this land find themselves agreeing with Africans of a million years ago, with Icelanders of a thousand years ago, with Siberians and Scandinavians and Eskimos of today, who live in close touch with a very demanding landscape. The values of the hard places of the world have come to us from the evolutionary origins of humanity, not from the civilizations created by the world's comfortable Mediterranean places. Alaskans live by patterns of belief and behavior that are millions of years old, when they live in harmony with their land. The innovations of fair weather civilizations seem inadequate and inappropriate by comparison.

Alaska's indigenous lifestyle is based upon aesthetic and philosophical values that are rooted in the evolutionary origins of mankind, not merely in the civilized centers of western art and thought. Alaskans have access to a powerful environment which can be absorbed within them, and which can be expressed with all the directness and all the immanent sense of reality that is inherent in the land itself. They have an opportunity to explore and perhaps to develop some fundamental truths about the human species which may not agree with what is usually taught in the academic disciplines called the "humanities." This is a place where the humanities should expand to include the natural history of our own and other species, in relation to the environments which have fed the growth of the human spirit. That does not mean that Alaskans should adopt an "ah, Wilderness" attitude, or that they should seek to "return to nature." Such ideas come generally from people who live in temperate cultures.

Henry David Thoreau is the acknowledged genius of the back-to-nature subgroup of the ecology movement. I see him living by

Walden Pond, contemplating nature. Then I see an Eskimo hunter, bending for hours at -40° F. over a pushup in the ice, waiting for a seal to appear. That, too, is a contemplation of nature, but Thoreau would never have understood it. What Thoreau saw in Walden Pond was his own reflection, I think, plus a beautiful fantasy world of nature being kind to mankind. He saw symbols in his pond. What does the Eskimo see? Well, with luck, he may or he may not see a concrete reality which he can eat, providing he is skillful enough. That, I think, is a more significant contemplation of nature. Maybe Alaskans don't love nature as Thoreau did, or as Wordsworth did, or as other romantics from temperate places say they do. Maybe they really hate it because it is always trying to kill them or to freeze off a toe, or the tip of a nose.

Nature in Alaska is a nature of power, not of comfort. It is a substantial reality that cannot and must not be ignored. Those who live attentively to its presence find their own power and reality there, too. Finding that is worth the pain. There is also a kind of love, but not the sentimental kind. It's more like living with some crazy Nordic god who is always ready to blast you if you stop living it, but who is essentially indifferent and doesn't care what happens to you.

Oil development is a threat to the Alaskan lifestyle in several ways. For one thing, it puts decisions in the hands of powerful people who are completely ignorant of this land — corporations, government officials, the "boomers." Inappropriate policies are likely to result, made by inappropriate people living in the wrong places. Another danger is that oil's influence might make Alaskan life too easy. It might insulate people with money and technology from the natural conditions of life here. Alaskans might come to resemble my friend in Fairbanks who boasted every spring that he had been through the entire winter without experiencing any temperature lower than 60° F. He went from his heated apartment to his heated garage and warmed up his car and drove to his heated garage at work, got into his heated elevator and went to his heated office. He spent an entire winter in Fairbanks without ever feeling cold air, just as New Yorkers often live a complete life without ever touching genuine earth.

Another threat from oil is that it may introduce ways of life that don't belong here. An example is the imposition of corporate structures, developed in the Mediterranean tradition, but now being applied to the Native communities of Alaska. We should worry when we hear that institutions derived from life in temperate climates, whether in Greece or India or Houston or wherever, are determining the fates of Alaskans. But more dangerous than any of these threats from oil development is the prospect that oil extraction may threaten the integrity of the Alaskan land itself, and with it the Alaskan lifestyle.

Alaskans have become expert at the art of responding to threats and dangers. They do not usually rush heroically to man the battlements or to ride proudly off into battle. No, they are more likely to apply craft and guile and imagination and inventiveness and wit and a strange sort of spiritual, psychological jujitsu, using their antagonist's momentum to save themselves. That's how they make it through winter, too. That part of the Alaskan lifestyle is not an ideology at all, but a strategy.

If there is hope for surviving the threats posed by rapid mineral development, it is based on the presumption that any people who can preserve themselves through winter should be able to handle fragile, dying beasts like oil companies or worn-out southern civilizations. Is the pipeline really a greater threat than winter is? I doubt it.

EARTH SONG

POETRY OF THE LAND: HUMOR AND HARD TIMES
William Kloefkorn

A lot of poets have written a lot of poems about the land. I conclude from this that the land must be worth writing about. Sometimes, of course, the land is used as a means to an end; the romantic, for example, uses the land as a way of expressing his own personal sense of delight or despair or despondency or joy or whatever. Minnesota Poet Joe Paddock, in a poem called "Black Energy," acknowledges the earth, the land, as "A mingling of untold billions of bodies / of plants and animals: / grasses of this prairie, / buffalo and antelope grazing down / into roots and back again / into the sun. / Birds and insects, their wings / still hum in this soil. / And this swarm drinks / sunlight and rain, / and rises again and again / into corn and beans / and flesh and bone. // The quick bodies of animals and men / risen / from this black energy." As "black energy," the land incorporates and transcends us all; mice and men, Texans and Nebraskans, become only a part of the recurrent energy that is the land. Walt Whitman, in "This Compost," wrote, "Behold this compost! behold it well! / The grass of spring covers the prairies, / The bean bursts noiselessly through the mould in the garden ... / Out of its little hill faithfully rise the potato's dark green leaves, / Out of its hill rises the yellow maizestalk, the lilacs bloom in the dooryards, / The summer growth is innocent and disdainful above all those strata of sour dead." Whitman goes perhaps a step further in "A Song of the Rolling Earth": "I swear there is no greatness or power that does not emulate those of the earth, / There can be no theory of any account unless it corroborate the theory of the earth, / No politics, song, religion, behavior, what not, is of account, unless it compare with the amplitude of the earth. / Unless it face the exactness, vitality, impartiality, rectitude of the earth." Kentucky Poet Wendell Berry sees himself as a part of the overall enrichment of the earth: "I am slowly falling into the fund of things ... / After death, willing or not, the body serves, / entering the earth. And so what was heaviest / most mute is at last raised up into song." Ralph Waldo Emerson's "Earth-Song," from his poem "Hamatreya," is an effort to show the extent to which man is puny if not pitiful when compared to the land:

"Mine and yours;
Mine, not yours.
Earth endures;
Stars abide —
Shine down in the old sea;
Old are the shores;
But where are the old men?
I who have seen much,
Such have I never seen.

"The lawyer's deed
Ran sure,
In tail,
To them, and to their heirs
Who shall succeed,
Without fail,
Forevermore.

"Here is the land,
Shaggy with wood,
With its old valley,
Mound and flood.
But the heritors?
Fled like the flood's foam.
And the lawyer, and the laws,
And the kingdom,
Clean swept herefrom.

"They called me theirs,
Who so controlled me;
Yet every one
Wished to stay, and is gone,
How am I theirs,
If they cannot hold me,
But I hold them?"

When I heard the Earth-song,
I was no longer brave;
My avarice cooled
Like lust in the chill of the grave.

These poets, and others, declare the worth and the dignity and the staying power of the earth. Most of them take themselves and their worthy subjects seriously, which is fine — though the subject of land, and of man's relationship to it, is not one that need always be approached with either a heavy heart or a heavy hand. Since the middle of the nineteenth century American writers have been able to take themselves and their acreage with a grain of salt. This was especially true of the comic journalists, through hardy souls like Seba Smith and Josh Billings and Artemus Ward and Johnson Jones Hooper and many others, who found at least a touch of humor in the most unfortunate of conditions and circumstances. This isn't an easy thing to do, sometimes — I'll be the first to admit it. We are a proud, stubborn, sometimes arrogant, often self-righteous people. God gave us this land, directed us to it, protected us — well, *some* of us — in the face of seastorm and wolf and Savage and blizzard and drought and flood, and this means of course that we have some type of celestial claim to the land, though God in his wisdom didn't actually give us a deed. So what we owned originally by divine right we now own, more or less, by legal title, which means that God is beginning to look more and more like a lawyer. Chaucer's Summoner is becoming commonplace: *"Questio quid juris"* — "The question is, what is the law?"

I borrowed several lines from Kansas Poet Bruce Cutler when I was looking for a prefatory note for my first collection of poems, *Alvin Turner As Farmer*. The lines are from a book-length narrative by Cutler called *A West Wind Rises*. They go like this:

> Only the man
> who gives himself whole-hide to land can know
> how absolute it is
> to own. Or lose.

Late in my book Alvin Turner wonders about this problem of ownership:

> To yield
> What you have never owned,
> Then call it loss:
> This is the turtle's puny voice
> The height of wilderness.
>
> Why is it then
> That the sweetest sound
> I know
> Is one unthrottled throat,
> Crying?

It is the "sweetest sound" because it is so undeniable, so intense; the farmer at this point knows that he is going to lose the land, and his lament is nothing if not genuine. I feel very close to Alvin Turner, probably because both of us had a Protestant fundamentalist upbringing that we can't get entirely away from. My grandmother said "How beautiful heaven must be!" out of one side of her mouth, while out of the other she asked the doctor for medicine enough to prolong her life here on this veil of tears for another fifteen or twenty minutes. Alvin Turner married such a woman (no one is perfect, especially when he is often at the mercy of his glands), though he was not himself much of an institutionalized Christian. Anyway, he manages occasionally to smile at himself, and at his circumstance, even in the face of death. And this I believe to be a healthy condition. Here are several poems from *Alvin Turner;* each to some extent suggests how the farmer keeps his perspective during times of stress.

(*Stress # 1: husband-wife quarrel*)

> New canvas for the combine:
> It had to be done,
> Though the boys' shoes turn to skin.
> Can't a woman understand
> A simple thing like that?
> Each man has his own machine
> To keep in tune, I say,
> And I don't like to think
> He has to sacrifice one vital cog.
>
> But somewhere the message gets confused,
> And I'm blamed if I can make it right.
>
> So the children walk our shards on bloody feet
> While father, fat on canvas, dissipates.
> She seems to see us so, at any rate,
> And when she sighs and gathers up her yard
> I try again.
>
> I love the boys like they were fanbelts,
> I say,
> And brand new.

(*Stress # 2: being called upon to pray at Thanksgiving dinner*)

108

friends that
fresh-braised pork
you're licking chops
to was on the
hoof a week ago
rooting rubbish
with the same
nostrils I chose
to fire the rifle bullets
into that act being
only one of god's
manifold mysterious
ways for which
on this november day
we all should probably
give thanks
amen!

(*Stress #3: disputing whether to have a child baptized; the first child died of pneumonia*)

Martha says that all the rivers
Run to the sea,
Yet the sea is not full.
I have trimmed a new wick,
And beside its even flame
Martha reads aloud,
Her voice clean as mopped linoleum.
Pshaw, I say, needling,
What has that to do with downspouts?

> (I know that she wants the baby baptized,
> And I don't really care, one way or the other.
> Our first child took her rebirth
> With her to the grave,
> So that I'd personally rather see
> The water on the corn, or not at all.
> But I'll not be muleheaded.)

She looks up briefly, not answering,
Then reads that there is no new thing
Under the sun. I nod,
Meaning that I shall arrange the baptism
For the earliest Sunday.

> (I wouldn't mention it
> In town at the feedstore,
> But Martha's voice by lamplight
> Is worth at least one waste of rain.)

(Stress #4: the bother of bringing up two young sons)

> *look boys*
> *I don't honestly know*
> *whether jesus wants either of you*
> *for a sunbeam you'll*
> *have to check with your*
> *mother if you must have*
> *my opinion though*
> *I'd guess he has*
> *plenty already like*
> *for instance that one*
> *there on the knifeblade*
> *which by midnight*
> *just might be*
> *sharp enough to saw*
> *lard if you two bandits*
> *will keep the grindstone*
> *wet*
> *you hear me?*

(Stress #5: difference of opinion about religion)

> Not even on the Sabbath
> Can we leave the chores to heaven.
> I mention this to Martha,
> She tosses off a smile, not breaking stride.
> It means we better hustle
> Or be late for Sunday school.
> Between breakfast and
> The stripping of the cows
> The house releases redolence.
> The boys smell of yesterday's homemade haircuts,
> Their talcum hovering like halos.
> Martha clouds the air with stout sachet.
> Into it all,
> Like a bull sideboarded for market,
> I stomp my barnyard boots,
> Throw water to my hair and face,
> Then towel it downward,
> Dripping from the elbows.
> The day, familiar as a necktie,
> Turns like an auger in a woodknot,
> And during the testimonials
> I knead my chinflesh into dough,
> Stanching sleep.
>
> I sometimes fail.
> Last Sunday in the center of the sermon

I tacked canvas to the hen-house windows.
Three roosters, shivering, applauded,
And I looked up to see
Christ like a pea-eyed whirlwind
Sitting on a buckboard.
Are you Job? he asked.
No, I said, he lives one farm to the north.
You'll know him by the pockmarks on his face,
And by the holy stitching through his mouth.
I invited the voice to dinner,
But before I heard an answer
Its form had grown comb and feathers.

I awoke to the singing of a strange salvation
And to the shaking of weekly hands.

These poems aren't thigh-slappers, but they reveal, I hope, an attitude, a frame of mind, a perspective that enables the persona to cope a little better with himself and with others — and with the land that is both his pride and his punishment.

We need such an attitude today in our poetry. It can serve to remind us that unlike the lower animals we can laugh at ourselves. Mark Twain noted that man is the only animal that blushes — or has reason to. He also noted, via Philip Traum, the "Mysterious Stranger," that man has one major plus in his otherwise minus-dominated repertoire — and that plus is laughter: " ... your race, in its poverty, has unquestionably one really effective weapon — laughter. Power, money, persuasion, supplication, persecution — these can lift at a colossal humbug — push it a little — weaken it a little, century by century; but only laughter can blow it to rags and atoms at a blast." Well, perhaps. But in any case, humor levels inhibitions — social, political, religious. It reminds us that we are fallible; it encourages humility. And in a number of ways it can warn us against errors that might very well engulf, if not destroy, us. Jim Hightower, for example, gives us a menu in his book *Eat Your Heart Out,* a menu calculated to cause us to do more than merely salivate. Our choices of salads: Tossed Salad of Lettuce by Dow Chemical, tomatoes by Gulf & Western, Avocado Salad by Superior Oil. Side dishes: Artichokes by Purex, Carrots by Tenneco, Potatoes by Boeing, Apple Sauce by American Brands, Deviled Eggs by Cargill, Olives by Zapata Oil. (I must confess, though, that one of the beverages, Citrus Juice by Pacific Lighting Corp., has its own

111

perverse appeal.) Hightower amuses me at the same time that he warns me; the poem begins in delight, as Robert Frost might agree, and ends in wisdom.

Perhaps I can illustrate this point more fully with a poem I wrote a couple of summers ago when the heat in Nebraska was so intense that even the Presbyterians were beginning to complain. (They were starting to take Pudd'nhead Wilson's advice: "when angry, count four; when very angry, swear.") Some of my colleagues were wondering when I was going to write a hot-weather poem, and finally, no thanks to either my colleagues or to the hot spell, I wrote one. I call it — appropriately, I believe — "Drought." Here is the way it goes:

DROUGHT

Nobody wears clothes any more,
not even the local virgin's
scarecrow.

The manikins in all the storefronts
have dropped their drawers
like so many hot potatoes.

One goat and three medium-sized children
have so far disappeared
down a split in the ground
behind the Champlin station.

Between two upright posts
a length of #9 wire
whines like a Baptist's prayer
in a depraved wind.

Ham and eggs for half price,
fresh off the cement grill
in front of Rocky's Cafe.

For one thin dime you can earn the privilege
of watching Roy Duncan start a fire
with his fingers.

Boll weevils gather like flies
wherever Vernon Ryan
elects to spit.

Even the preacher's mistress
has given up the show,
her high heels arrested

in the pitch of the pavement,
her lipstick running like chokecherry
down the cleft of her chin.

It's no use:
Hell has moved her headquarters
into southeastern Nebraska.

Far into the night the last of the dogs
keeps everyone in town awake
with its decision
not to bark.

Well, it was uncommonly warm that summer, and I don't doubt
that another summer will come along, sooner or later, and be
equally warm. And when such a summer occurs, we are reminded
not only of our fallibility, but also of our low tolerance for pain and
discomfort. We whine. What *are* we going to do if this infernal heat
doesn't let up? Well, we are going to remain hot. What *are* we going
to do if Iran doesn't get its daily production of oil back up to at
least six million barrels per day? Well, we might have to sell one of
our six family cars. We depend upon Iran for more things than we
want to admit, and if that country withheld enough oil from us,
and for a long period of time, we might even be able to credit her
with getting our highway and byway deaths under 50,000 per year.

If it isn't one thing, all of our grandparents used to say, it's another: snow, ice, wind, hail, frost, rain, politicians. I grew up in
southcentral Kansas, where sometimes it forgot to rain. Then once
its memory got jolted, and it did rain, it forgot to stop. In the following poem, from *loony,* the boys in the pool hall are sitting out
such a rain, playing pool and cards and dominoes and drinking
more than their fair share of red beer. One of the principals is a fellow named Delbert Garlow, a man whose eyes are permanently
crossed because, according to loony, Delbert drinks too much of
his own home-brew. And perhaps he does. In any case, the rain is
falling, the boys in the pool hall are passing the time of day, and
Delbert Garlow puts in his two cents' worth. Loony quotes and
paraphrases Delbert as best he can:

Delbert Garlow talks
on and on and on
about the rain,

says that already the mud is so deep
that all his shorter hogs
are disappearing.
Delbert talks with his eyes crossed,
as if for luck:
says where is that
God damn Noah, anyhow,
now that we need him?
Delbert sits
far tilted back
like danger
in his chair,
eating a new cigar.
In front of him
his hands are placing dominoes
in the shape of a tapered wall.
Delbert, who is keeping score,
says that the only thing
a man can do,
unless he's a duck,
is stick his finger in the nearest hole.

Now about stoicism I feel a keen ambivalence. I don't really want to wait grinning for Iran to reduce the number of American traffic deaths; I prefer the retaining of a sensible speed limit, the manufacturing of automobiles that are considerably safer. And I'm likewise reluctant to wait on the God of Moisture either to send or to withhold its showers, though I appreciate the Freudian overtones of Delbert's quest for "the nearest hole"; even so, I'd prefer a damn here and there, here and there an irrigation sprinkler. It is terribly difficult, though, to know when to be stoic and when to act — and, if action is taken, how far to take it. At the present time, for example, I am not convinced that we need to damn the Niobrara River in Nebraska, and I'm beginning to wonder if some of the hugest of the irrigation systems might not be lowering our water reserves to a dangerous level. The picture becomes complex, one befuddled with such items as greed and fear and gross national product and altruism and what have you.

The poet's role in all of this is tough to define. I believe that he should write out of that sense of place that is most real and most vital to him, and that he should not become unduly angry — angry, that is, to the point that he becomes propagandistic. This implies, I hope, that he should not only keep his f-a-c-u-l-t-i-e-s intact, but also his sense of humor. Poets make poor propagandists, Philip

114

Freneau and Robert Bly to the contrary notwithstanding; the wheel that squeaks the loudest often gets a substitute for grease. The poet of course can hit hard, but his blows usually come from the north-northwest; he tells the truth, but (as Emily Dickinson admonishes) he tells it "slant." Richard Brautigan, for example, amuses with his hard-hitting irony in "All Watched Over by Machines of Loving Grace":

> I like to think (and
> the sooner the better!)
> of a cybernetic meadow
> where mammals and computers
> live together in mutually
> programming harmony
> like pure water
> touching clear sky.
>
> I like to think
> (right now, please!)
> of a cybernetic forest
> filled with pines and electronics
> where deer stroll peacefully
> past computers
> as if they were flowers
> with spinning blossoms.
>
> I like to think
> (it has to be!)
> of a cybernetic ecology
> where we are free of our labors
> and joined back to nature,
> returned to our mammal
> brothers and sisters,
> and all watched over
> by machines of loving grace.

The poem at once terrifies and tickles. Brautigan gives us a picture of the lion and the lamb lying peacefully together, but the lion, as it turns out, has been replaced by "machines of loving grace." The poem is frightening and amusing because Brautigan controls his irony, keeps his voice calm (except for the measured outbursts within parentheses). And the reader stands warned.

Brautigan doesn't give us answers. Most poets don't. Like dramatists (many dramatists, anyway), poets try to scratch the surface, leaving practical solutions to more practical minds. (My own definition of a poem is this: words that nibble at the edge of something vast. The definition is predicated upon my belief that it is better to have nibbled, and lost, than never to have nibbled at all.) Or the poet gives us an effect while hinting at the cause. Consider the way that Archibald MacLeish ends his poem "Empire Builders":

> They screwed her scrawny and gaunt with their seven-year panics:
> They bought her back on their mortgages old-whore-cheap:
> They fattened their bonds at her breasts till the thin blood ran from
> them.
> Men have forgotten how full clear and deep
> The Yellowstone moved on the gravel and the grass grew
> When the land lay waiting for her westward people!

The ending of this poem is about as amusing as a frontal lobotomy. Yet MacLeish began the poem in a rather amusing way, giving the reader a brief description of five panels, each of which depicts an American millionaire, all of which are presented by the museum attendant. The attendant says this, for example, of Commodore Vanderbilt:

> This is Commodore Vanderbilt making America:
> Mister-Vanderbilt-is-eliminating-the-short-interest-in-Hudson:
> Observe the carving on the rocking chair.

The attendant, who opens with the line, "This is *The Making of America in Five Panels,*" has memorized his speeches well, and we chuckle at his simplistic attitudes; but by the time we reach the end of the poem, we note the extent to which the museum, the attendant included, has pigeonholed and glossed the history of the development of America. The poem smiles its way to tears. If offers no direct solutions, but implicit in its satire is a call fro reassessment, if not action.

But hindsight, we know, is easier than foresight; it is difficult to take appropriate and correct action at the time it should be taken. Consider, for example, the plight of the southcentral Kansas basketball hopeful who in the late 1940's had to play the game wearing cotton athletic socks, the type that didn't keep their shape very long, the type that worked their way down into the tennis shoes after a quarter or so of scrimmage. The player at that point had the option of pulling up his socks or learning to run on two balls of cotton bunched up under his heels. Bright fellows might have taped the socks to the legs; brighter fellows might have tried out for cheerleader; the brightest of all might have sat in the stands and chewed popcorn or a sweetheart's earlobe. Back home, most of us learned to run on the balls of cotton. We called it "Making Do":

MAKING DO

The tops of all the sweatsocks
on the Cunningham high school gym
are disappearing,
are bunching downward
into damp discolored lumps
while the boys are practicing.

Who do not notice, or, noticing,
can not care.
Who have seen worse,
or have heard about it,
from a loved one or neighbor.
Elmira Bateman, for example,
a pin in her hip like a stovebolt,
whistles half the day
at gathering a dozen eggs.
Leroy Shannon waltzes the same tincan
all the way to the drugstore
with his mulberry leg.
Sadie Henderson has been half a century
at doctoring her bloody corns
with brown cotton hose
and a rayon smile.

It is not well to whine.
Thus the boys at practice
on the Cunningham High School gym
grin and leap on,
the tops of their sweatsocks
disappearing,
bunching downward
into the sweet malignant lumps
of precedent.

Many of our problems today exist because we are being dictated to from someone's outmoded grave. Others exist, or are being born, because we place personal greed over the welfare of the general population and its posterity. A while back I tried to imagine what would happen if some hotshot fisherman managed to catch the very last catfish in all the world. This is a somewhat ridiculous premise, I reckon, because the catfish (at least in Nebraska, at least in the Loup River) is alive and well and thriving. But just for the hell of it I granted the premise: an aspiring fisherman has just latched on to the very last catfish in the cosmos. Here is what he does — in a poem I call "with the rib of a mouse tied to the end of a string ludi jr catches the last of the world's great catfish":

I can see it in his one good eye
in the way he manages
always to turn it
to be facing me

as much as to say
look:
I am the last of the world's great catfish
destroy me and nowhere ever
can there be another

and from behind the cord
that lines his lip
does ludi jr wrestle free the hood
a smell of blood and meat and bone
trailing the barb

but the hand at the end
of ludi jr's mind
does not relent
except to kill and skin
and clean and eat
the beautiful flesh
of the last of the world's great catfish

such a course of action being
in this scheme of things
the only way to reign:
to be the very last
and thus the highest
of the world's great catfish

fishermen

I hope things never come to this; I hope that we can make the best of our rivers at the same time that we preserve the catfish. There must be a satisfactory middle ground somehwere, and we must find it. Too often "in this scheme of things / the only way to reign" is to destroy without replacing, and I personally don't see this as a very reasonable solution. I'm not much in favor of a "cybernetic meadow" where all of us at last are "watched over / by machines of loving grace," but I don't want to toss the baby out with the bathwater, either, if I may offer a metaphor that isn't entirely original. I not only want to have my cake and eat it, too, but I want to watch it and admire it and feel its texture — all at the same time.

I did this in a sense several summers ago when Nebraska produced one of its bumper corn crops. I found myself one bright clear day in the middle of a cornfield near Greenwood, a small town just a stone's throw east of Lincoln. The corn was as high as an elephant's eye; the acreage was absolutely free of weeds and bugs; and the farmer, who was eating well that year, was glandular with pride. I asked him how much he spent to keep the field (which was enormous) so clean. He gave me a figure that caused me to suck and to swallow a large quantity of air. So whatever happened to all the hard times, anyway? Well, they come and they go. They are always with us. And they are always moving on. A time to reap, and a time to sow. To love and to die. And if things go well, said the farmer, I think I can do even better next year.

And it occurred to me that this scene had been made possible because of an agricultural-industrial system too complex to be understood or accounted for or changed, for better or for worse, overnight. And I was struck too with the farmer's persistence, with his hope, with his potential greed. Later, in my dreams, I saw the farmer tossing in his dreams, unable to sleep because one lone bug had managed to escape his pesticides. The next day I wrote the following poem, one I call "Otoe County in Nebraska" (it wasn't in fact Otoe County, but I like the sound of Otoe).

OTOE COUNTY IN NEBRASKA

On the run is the Otoe County corn rootworm,
overcome by laboratories;
who have purpled the soil with nuggets enough
to deter the deepest scavenger.
Thus as you drive the plush curvaceous trails
of Otoe County
you can sense the rootworm's grim retreat —
the dirty little no good
crop killing bugger
hightailing it for Kansas and Oklahoma,

for south Texas,
through Mexico
to a tip in Yucatan
from which it can throw itself
for mercy into the sea.
You can imagine it going without breakfast,
halfway now across the Caribbean,
dogpaddling its hundred thousand legs
to maintain a slim distance
between its life's little juice
and the laboratories that,
running at full throttle with periscope up,
cannot unlock their hatches until that
last little juice has been spilled.

Meanwhile, back in Otoe County,
the cornrows rise corpulent as green trees.
In a red Volkswagen you are a snail, hunched and alien and
terribly humble.

This magnificence was the result of several forces: the farmer's skills, shipbuilders, adequate sunlight and moisture, laboratories (Dow Chemical, say), the good folks down at Volkswagen. The lion and the lamb make hay together. The result: cornrows that "rise corpulent as green trees," which in turn reduce the onlooker to "a snail, / hunched and alien and terribly humble."

My point at this point is that in order to have our cake and eat it too we must learn to work with Dow Chemical and others, even including the hard-headed (of whom I am one) Germans, and/or their equivalents.

One rather major roadblock sits in the way: people. When we talk about "poetry of the land" we must likewise talk about the people who contend with the land; when we talk about "humor and hard times," we must talk about the people who experience the hard times. Alexander Pope called man "The glory, jest, and riddle of the world." The Brobdingnagian king in Jonathan Swift's *Gulliver's Travels* calls us, by way of Gulliver, "the most pernicious race of little odious vermin that nature ever suffered to crawl upon the surface of the earth." At the moment I'm personally not all that pessimistic, though I would like to single out two types of people who don't do much to make things better. The first is the one who is forever indecisive. I chose a woman named Elsie Martin to represent this type, and to present her I invented a small-town pool-hall philosopher and spitter and whistler whom I call Stocker. Here is what Stocker says about indecision — by way of Elsie Martin:

ELSIE MARTIN

She's six of one, half a dozen of another,
According to Stocker:
Not a bad looker, for a widowwoman,
But her face so knobbed with indecision
You'd swear she has hemorrhoids.
Heard of another case just like her,
He said,
Who starved to death in a grocery store,
Comparing labels.
Always and forever between a rock and a hard place —
Not fishing, quite,
And not quite cutting bait.
So precisely between the devil
And the deep blue sea
That she lives with one foot in heaven
And the other in hot water.
Split her right down the middle,
Stocker said,
And it wouldn't make a dime's worth of difference
Which half you reached for.

Sometimes this person does not actually starve to death in the midst of plenty; instead, the individual waits until it is too late, then with a last-ditch effort tries to make up for lost time by giving away material possessions. I call this person "Dollard," which is just one letter removed from "Dollar," and again I permit Stocker to do most of the critical talking:

DOLLARD

Dollard is beginning to give
himself away,
now not only in bits and pieces:

but gone now the chimes and the radio,
the curtains and the chairs,
the rugs and lampshades

and the Chevrolet.
And there are wide silent gaps now
all up and down

the old man's armory.
Yesterday, in the pool hall,
he gave as chips the first nails

crowbarred from his house.
This morning, in Bake's Cafe,
he handed Bake a watch, a billfold,

and a wedding ring.
Tomorrow, according to Stocker,
he'll shed his boots and his shirt

and his overalls:
next week, likely as not,
his hair and his eyebrows,

scattering locks.
Generous now to a fault,
Stocker says,

Christ on his way uphill,
forewarned and lonely
and desperate for a cross.

That isn't a very humorous poem, is it? I'm sorry. I'm neglecting my own advice — namely, don't be afraid to take things, however serious they might be in and of themselves, with a grain of salt.

The other type is the individual who talks and acts without bothering to become informed, the one who is much flicker but little flame. I name this person Mrs. Wilma Hunt, and just one more time I'll call upon Stocker to do the color commentary.

MRS. WILMA HUNT

Stocker said the air that came from
Mrs. Wilma Hunt
Had no more teeth in it
Than prohibition.
He knew more than one woman just like that, he said,
Most of them sired no doubt
By dreams of cyclones.
Mrs. Wilma Hunt knew everything
There was to know
About nothing.
According to Stocker,
As if someone some time or other, he said,
Had twisted her one notch too tight,
Stripping the threads,

So that now she's like a cattle truck
On its way home,
The wind whistling Dixie
Through the slats of her sideboards,
The whole kit and caboodle
Going hellbent for election,
As Stocker put it,
But running empty.

My points are these: the land, including the people who work
with the land, is worth writing about; the writer, certainly including
the poet, should write out of that sense of place (or places) which
for him is most real and most vital (I appreciate what Michigan
Poet John Woods says about this: "I like a poem which has one
foot firmly planted on the earth, one foot so heavily put down that
it doesn't matter where the other foot has wings for"); and, finally,
the writer (again with an emphasis upon the poet) should not always take himself and/or his subject so seriously that he becomes a
propagandist or a preacher. He should keep in mind that there are
three times when his sense of humor should be intact: 1) when the
times are hard, 2) when the times are soft, and 3) when the times
are in between.

I want to conclude by talking briefly about a matter that isn't entirely relevant to the title of these ramblings, though I consider it to
be at least a second cousin. I call it "Poetry of the Land: Humor
and *Good* Times." It seems to me that the poet should learn to feel
good when he is feeling good, and that he should not hesitate to
share this joy with others — especially if the joy derives from the
land. I realize that for some of us it isn't discreet to sing or shout or
click our heels this side of heaven, but once in a while I find it un-
natural not to. I drive the valley of the Platte River, I lose my teeth,
such as they are, in a winesap apple at Nebraska City, I push my
fingers into a hundred million million kernels of hybrid seed not far
from Bennett, I look down from my seat in a United jet and see for
the first time the first sign of an ancient and a new frontier called
Alaska, and the final two lines of a poem come to mind: "Enough
almost by god to make a fellow / Not ashamed to worship." I go to
North Platte, Nebraska, where in the saloon at the Ramada Inn I
watch a cowgirl lasso and break a greenhorn; I enter a hog-calling
contest, and win it, and go on the proclaim it in a poem that admits

123

that without hogs the victory would not have been possible. I watch
Alvin Turner, on a good autumn day, proclaim

> This morning I am dizzy
> With the plumb brown evidence of fall.
> The granary is full.
> The bucket at the cistern glints its use.
> The baby is solid as a tractor lug.
> In the kitchen
> Martha glows fuller than her cookstove's fire.
> I want a dozen pancakes,
> Ma'am,
> A ton of sausage,
> Half a crate of eggs,
> Some oatmeal and a loaf of toast.
> Feed me,
> Woman,
> Then kindly step back!
>
> I intend to do some pretty damn fancy whistling
> While I slop the hogs.

On a day that is not altogether good, I hear Alvin Turner accept,
with pride and a dash of delight, the bitter and the sweet:

> I am a dirt farmer
> Who dreams of poetry.
> Is that so strange? Is anything?
> I have bent myself thankfully
> Over the heat of cowchips.
> When the lespedeza flowers
> I breathe its blooms.
> The calf I winch to birth
> Grows legs like oaks to graze on,
> And stuck hogs bleed for breakfasts.
> This morning at milking
> I kissed the cow's warm flank
> And she kicked the milk to froth beneath my knees.
> I forgave her,
> Then cried with the cats,
> Now the manure is in bloom,
> Thistles defend the driveway,
> And corncobs gird the mud beneath my boots,
> Plotting harvests,
> I roam my acreage like a sweet spy.

I am saying that it might be as difficult for us to sing gracefully
of good times as it is for us to cope gracefully with the bad ones.

One more example and I'll shut up. In late October of last year I drove from Lincoln to Anselmo, to the Joe Johnson ranch near Anselmo, where I was to meet a covey of poets for a Saturday session. (I hope you Alaskans have such coveys. They can do a lot for poetry, for themselves and others, for the area in which they write.) I left on Friday afternoon, driving a Nebraska State automobile and munching a modest bag of Spanish peanuts. I was moving into a lowering sun, and the day was splendid — bright, crisp, windless. All along the way the farmers were finishing their grain harvest; the countryside was rife with corn and maize and stubble and pheasants. I felt good. I turned off the interstate onto a small highway, and the scenery improved, came closer, intensified. I crossed a series of creeks, all of them branches of a stream named "Mud Creek," all of the branches neatly and unashamedly posted "Mud Creek." I drove through Ravenna, the cheese capitol of southcentral Nebraska; I stopped for a beer at Hazard; I drove through and skirted a dozen other towns, all of them carrying names that suggested nothing short of poetry. In the midst of all this I saw a shabby man-made sign, blue and white, declaring "God loves you." It was too much. Here I was, touring the heart of paradise, and, if I didn't believe it or have the sensibility to feel it, I had a gaudy sign to spell it out for me.

I stayed that night in a ramshackle hotel in Broken Bow, where I wrote the following poem. It is called "Along Highway 2 in Central Nebraska":

> With the aid of a late October sun
> the witnesses along Highway 2,
> in Central Nebraska,
> have sworn to tell the truth,
> the whole truth,
> and nothing but.
>
> Six miles east of Sweetwater,
> between the first two branches
> of Mud Creek,
> the news from its longsuffering sign
> slips out:
> God loves you.
> Ravenna blushes the color of cheese
> in the general direction
> of Berwyn and Litchfield and Mason City,

of Little Rhino's Bar & Grill in Ansley.

In the Hazard (Pop. 70) Cafe
the choicest hog
in all of Sherman County
smiles up and into the teeth
of a Burlington Northern engineer.

All of the herefords at Cairo
have been polled,
with only a slim majority
in favor.

The Homeward Trail Bible Camp,
closed for the season,
is overrun with hawks and mice,
and neglected handsaws,
with the beasts of the fields
and their pagan children.

Grain wagons. Cottonwoods.
Alfalfa. Haybales. Stubble.
The slow-motion movement
of discs disappearing
in the soil.

The truth is,
the truth lies back there somewhere
in the bulrushes
between Mud Creek and Sweetwater.

So golly Moses, God,
what can a poor misguided city boy,
in the midst of all this various proof,
say, or do?

Well,

1) he can withdraw all his money
from the Custer County Savings and Loan in Broken Bow;
2) in the Nutshell Lounge
he can wash down his order of mountain oysters
with a schooner of cold Blue Ribbon beer;
3) he can (hell's-fire, Lord, by now it should be obvious),
he can love you, too.

All of us are a part of Joe Paddock's "Black Energy," 'a mingling
of untold billions of bodies ... (that) rise again and again / into
corn and beans / and flesh and bone." We are Whitman's compost,

126

"the grass of spring [that] covers the prairies." Meanwhile, as poets and painters, as teachers and students and laborers and technicians, let us work with a sense both of direction and of humor to keep the land from going entirely sour before its own sweet time.

POETRY, COMMUNITY & CLIMAX
Gary Snyder

I

I WROTE a small piece ten years ago called "Poetry and the Primitive." It was subtitled "Poetry as an ecological survival technique." In a brisk and simple way, I was trying to indicate what modern people might want to learn and use from the way poetry/song works in a strong, self-contained pre-literate society. I have also spoken of poetry's function as an occasional voice for the non-human rising within the human realm, and the value of that. Survival.

But it's clear now that survival is not exactly the problem. Not for human beings, who will survive come hell or high water — and both may — to find themselves sole operators of the equipment on a planet where vertebrate evolution has come to an end. Clouds of waterfowl, herds of bison, great whales in the ocean, will be — almost are — myths from the dream-time. As is, already, "the primitive" in any virgin sense of the term. Biological diversity, and the integrity of organic evolution on this planet, is where I take my stand: not a large pretentious stand, but a straightforward feet-on-the-ground stand, like my grandmother nursing her snapdragons and trying at grafting apples. It's also inevitably the stand of the poet, child of the Muse, singer of saneness and weaver of rich fabric to delight the mind with possibilities opening both inward and outward.

There is a huge investment in this nation: bridges, railway tracks, freeways, downtown office buildings, airports, aircraft carriers, miles of subdivisions, docks, ore-carriers, factories. All that belongs to somebody, and they don't want to see it become useless, unprofitable, obsolete. In strict terms of cash flow and energy flow it still works, but the hidden costs are enormous and those who pay the cost are not the owners. I'm speaking of course not only of human alienation but air and water, stands of trees, and all the larger, more specialized, rarer birds and animals of the world who pay the cost of "America" with their bodies — as mentioned above. To keep this investment working, the several thousand individuals who own it have about convinced the rest of us that we are equal owners with them of it; using language like "don't turn out the lights," "let's not go back to the stone age," and "you've worked hard for what you got, don't lose it now." Their investment requires continual growth, or it falters; and a "steady state economy" — "small is beautiful" are terrifying concepts for them because without growth, the gross inequalities in the distribution of wealth in this land would become starkly clear. From this it's evident that the future of capitalism and perhaps all industrial society is intimately staked on the question of nuclear energy — no other way to keep up growth. This leads to the disastrous fast breeder reactor (which is not dead yet by a long shot), and the fast breeder leads to a police state. But food shortages may bring it down even before energy shortages — the loss of soils and the growing inefficiencies of chemical fertilizers.

I repeat this well-known information to remind us, then, that monoculture heavy industry television automobile culture is not an ongoing accident; it is deliberately fostered. Any remnant city neighborhood of good cheer and old friendships, or farming community that "wants to stay the way it is" are threats to the investment. Without knowing it, little old ladies in tennis shoes who work to save Whooping Cranes are enemies of the state, along with other more flamboyant figures. I guess there are revolutionaries who still hope for their own kind of monocultural industrial utopia, however. And there are some for whom alienation is a way of life, an end in itself. It's helpful to remember that what we'd hope for on the planet is creativity and sanity, conviviality, the real work of our hands and minds: those apples and snapdragons. Existential *angst* won't go away nohow, if that's how you get your energy.

Although it's clear that we cannot again have seamless primitive cultures, or the purity of the archaic, we can have neighborhood and community. Communities strong in their sense of place, proud and aware of local and special qualities, creating to some extent their own cultural forms, not humble or subservient in the face of some "high cultural" over-funded art form or set of values, are in fact what one healthy side of their original American vision was about. They are also, now, critical to "ecological survival." No amount of well-meaning environmental legislation will halt the biological holocaust without people who live where they are and work with their neighbors, taking responsibility for their place, and *seeing to it:* to be inhabitants, and to not retreat. We feel this to be starting in America: a mosaic of city neighborhoods, small towns, and rural places where people are digging in and saying "if not now when? if not here, where?" This trend includes many sorts of persons, some of whom are simply looking out for themselves and finding a better place to live. The process becomes educational, and even revolutionary, when one becomes aware of the responsibility that goes with "rootedness" and the way the cards are stacked against it; we live in a system that rewards those who leap for the quick profit and penalizes those who would do things carefully with an eye to quality. Decentralization could start with food production. Old/new style biologically sophisticated farming doesn't imply total local self-sufficiency, but at least the capacity to provide food and fiber needs within a framework of two or three hundred miles. Then come new definitions of territory and region, and fresh ways to see local government limits — watershed politics, bio-region consciousness. Sense of community begins to include woodpeckers and cottontails. Decentralization includes the decentralization of "culture," of poetry.

II

Now to speak of 25 years of poetry readings in the U.S. When I was working on the docks in San Francisco and occasionally taking night courses in conversational Japanese around '52 or '53, writing poems and sending them off to magazines, *Kenyon Review,* and *Hudson Review* and *Partisan,* and getting them back, we had no sense of a community of poets and even less of an audience. Kenneth Rexroth held open house in his apartment on Friday evenings, and four or five or sometimes ten people might drop by; some out of an old Italian anarchist group, some from the filmmakers and artists circles of the Bay Area. In 1954 I knew virtually every poet, filmmaker and artist in the region. I hardly know who works in Berkeley anymore, let alone the rest.

In 1955 because Allen Ginsberg and Philip Whalen, Michael McClure, Philip Lamantia and several others, and myself, found ourselves with large numbers of unpublished poems on our hands, it occurred to us to give a poetry reading. It was like holding a sale. In those days all we ever thought of doing with poetry was to get it published; we didn't know who saw it, and didn't think to offer it up publicly. But we went ahead and organized a poetry reading. We did have a model or two; Dylan Thomas had passed through a year before; Ted Roethke had come down from Seattle and read; the San Francisco poetry center had organized a few readings in five or six years. Still, poetry readings were definitely not a part of the cultural and social landscape. That reading held in November 1955 in a space borrowed from an art gallery was a curious kind of turning point in American poetry. It succeeded beyond our wildest thoughts. In fact, we weren't even thinking of success; we were just trying to invite some friends and potential friends, and we borrowed a mailing list from the art gallery and sent out maybe two hundred postcards. Poetry suddenly seemed useful in 1955 San Francisco. From that day to this, there has never been a week without a reading in the Bay Area — actually more like three a night, counting all the coffee shops, plus schools, the art museum, the aquarium, and the zoo. Those early readings led to publication for some. *Howl* became the second book in Lawrence's Pocket Poets series, and Allen's extensive early readings all over the United States began to draw audiences of a size not seen before. Kerouac's novels were published, and the "beat generation" was launched. Allen was to a great extent responsible for generating the excitement, but a number of other poets (myself not among them because I had gone to Japan) travelled widely over the United States landing like crows first in coffee houses and later becoming gradually accepted more and more into the network of universities.

One thing that was clearly an error in the mentality of the early fifties literary world was the idea that poetry cannot have an audience, and indeed that it was a little shameful if a poem was too popular. There are people who still believe that, incidentally. There was also the defeatist attitude that "we live in a philistine culture" and no one is interested in art anyway, so we'll just write to each other. My generation found that by boldly, to put it bluntly, having something to say, helped with audiences. It also should be apparent that one is not *owed* an audience by the culture; but one can indeed go out and try to build an audience. Building that audience is done in part by going on the road and using your voice and your body to put the poems out there; and to speak to the people's condition, as the Quakers would say, to speak to the conditions of your own times, and not worry about posterity. If you speak to the condition of your times with some accuracy and intention, then it may speak to the future, too. If it doesn't, fine, we live in the present. So poetry readings as a new cultural form enhanced and strengthened poetry itself, and the role of the poet. They also taught us that poetry really is an oral art. It would be fascinating to undertake an examination of how poetry of the last 20 years has been shaped by the feedback that comes with reading in front of people. Poems go through revisions, adaptations and enhancements following on the sense of how audiences have been hearing you. So there is a communal aspect to the evolution of the art. Does this mean that poets, knowing that they were writing for an audience, might have catered to that possibility? Sure. But it also means that audiences have come up to the possibility to hearing better over the years. My experience is that the latter tends to be the case and that audiences have grown in maturity and the poetry with them. With a skilled audience, such as you often find in New York or San Francisco (and recently in Midwestern cities like Minneapolis), the poet knows that he/she can try for more, and really push it to the difficult, the complex, the outrageous, and see where the mind of the people will go.

This practice of poetry reading has had an effect on the poets who were quite content to regard poetry as a written art that sits on a printed page and belongs in libraries, too. They have been forced to actually learn how to read poetry aloud better out of sheer competition if nothing else. There are economic rewards involved.

Poetry belongs to everybody, but there are always a few skilled raconteurs or creators or singers, and we live in a time in which the individual actor or creator is particularly valued. The art wouldn't die out if we lost track of the name of the fellow who made it up, though, and the fact that we don't know the names of the men or women who made the songs in the past doesn't really matter.

All of this goes one more step, then, to a conscious concern and interest on the part of some poets in the actual performance skills of pre-literate people. My own studies in anthropology, linguistics, and oral literature, brought me to the realization that the performance, in a group context, is the pinnacle of poetic activity and precision, and we have yet to develop the possibilities of that circle with music, dance and drama in their original archaic poetic relationship. The Ainu singers of Hokkaido chant their long epic stories to a beat. The güslars of southern Yugoslavia use a little dulcimer-like stringed instrument. No wonder we say "lyric poetry" — they used to sing with a lyre. Most of the songs that you hear on the country and western hit parade are in good old English ballad meter, showing that the ballad is time to come. Other examples, simple examples: Robert Bly knows almost all his poems by heart and Roethke knew his. Reciting from memory (which I can't do) liberates your hands and mind for the performance — liberates your eyes. No drama, with its aristocratic spareness and simplicity, could be another model. Percussive, almost non-melodic music is very strong; a bare stage is all you need.

In this era of light shows, huge movie screens, and quadraphonic sound systems, it is striking that an audience will still come to hear a plain, ordinary unaugmented human being using nothing but voice and language. That tells us that people do appreciate the compression, the elegance, and the myriad imageries that come out of this art of distilling language and giving it measure which is called poetry.

III

The next step then is to ask what has a more public poetry done for the possibility of community? The modern poetry audience has a certain kind of network associated with it. Everywhere I go I meet people I know — from one corner of the United States to the other I never give a reading anymore but at least one person comes out of the audience, an old friend. A dozen other people that I haven't met before step up to tell me about how they are riding their horses or growing sunflowers somewhere, or are in the middle of making a Zendo inside an old building downtown. It's a fine exchange of news and information, and also the reaffirmation of a certain set of interests to which I (among others) speak. The community that is called together by such events is not just literary. It's interesting to see, then, that the universities have served as community halls, public space, that draw out people from beyond the immediate academic world. In other times and places such public spaces have been river beds — which is no man's land — where the gypsies and the travelling drama companies are allowed to put up their tents, or where the homeless samurai are allowed to act out their final duels with each other and nobody cares — it might be river beds, it might be the streets, or temples and churches — or in the tantric tradition of late medieval north India, some groups met in cemeteries.

What is this network of interests and old friends I speak of? None other than that branch of the stalwart counter-culture that has consistently found value and inspiration in poetry, and intellectual excitement in watching the unfolding of twentieth-century poetics. Also certain sets of values have been — in recent decades — more clearly stated in poetry than any other medium. (Other post-World War II cultural branches are primarily affiliated to music; some to more specific and intellectual formulated political or religious ideologies; a few go directly to crafts, or to gardening.) Anyway: the people who found each other via poetry readings in the late fifties and sixties produced another generation of poets who were committed to an oral poetics and a non-elite vision of communicating to larger and more diverse audiences. There are roughly three shoots from that root. I'll call them the dealers, the home-growers, and the ethno-botanists.

The "dealers" came in part with the growth of a certain academic and social acceptance of new poets and their readings, which led to the poetry policies of the NEA; the founding of the little magazines and small presses support organizations, the poets-in-the-schools programs, and on the academic side, several MFA-in-writing programs at several universities; workshops in poetry. At this point, via the poets-in-the-schools programs in particular, twentieth-century poetry began to find its way into ordinary American communities. The programs employed people who had gotten their MFA or a little book published (through a small press, with federal aid often) — and put them into high schools or grade schools, doing creative work, creative word playfulness, image playfulness; generating imagination and spontaneity among school children whose usual teachers couldn't. I consider this quite valid as a mode of poetic imagination and practice in its broadest sense filtering down through the population. The school districts themselves, after some resistance, began to accept the possibilities of poets and other artists doing local residencies. For every horror story of a brought-in poet reading a poem to the sixth grade with the word "penis" in it, there are countless unadvertised little openings of voice and eye as children got that quick view of playfulness, of the flexibility and power of their own mind and mother-tongue. I've watched this at work in my own school district, which is rural and short on money, but has backed the artists in schools as far as it could. In fact this school district (and many others) has chosen to keep arts programs going even after state or federal funding is withdrawn. One local poet found that what the children needed first was an introduction to the basic sense of story and of lore. He became the master of lore, myth, and word-hoard for the whole district. By much research and imagination, he provided, following the calendar and seasons, the true information — as story — about what Easter, May Day, Christmas, Hanukkah, Halloween, and Lammas are about. Neither the parents nor the school teachers in most cases could provide this fundamental lore of their own culture to the children. The poet was Steve Sanfield, doing the work of mythographer to the community in the ancient way.

The "home-growers" (and the above folks often overlap with this) are those poets who themselves live in a place with some intention of staying there — and begin to find their poetry playing a useful role in the daily life of the neighborhood. Poetry as a tool, a set or trap to catch and present; a sharp edge; a medicine, or the little awl that unties knots. Who are these poets? I haven't heard of most of them, neither have you; perhaps we never will. The mandarins of empire-culture arts organizations in the U.S. might worry about little-known poets working in the schools, because they are afraid of a decline in "standards of quality." I think I am second to none in my devotion to Quality; I throw myself at the lotus feet of Quality and shiver at the least tremor of her crescent-moon eyebrow. What they really fear is losing control over the setting of standards. But there is room for many singers, and not everyone need aspire to national-level publication, national reputation. The United States is, bio-regionally speaking, too large to ever be a comprehensible social entity except as maintained at great expense and effort via the media and bureaucracy. The price people pay for living in the production called American society is that they are condemned to continually watch television and read newspapers to know "what's happening," and thus they have no time to play with their own children or get to know the neighbors or birds or plants or seasons. What a dreadful cost! This explains why I do not even try to keep up with what's going on in nation-wide poetry publishing. We are talking about real culture now, the culture that things *grow* in, and not the laboratory strains of seeds that lead to national reputation. Poetry is written and read for real people: it should be part of the gatherings where we make decisions about what to do about uncontrolled growth, or local power-plants, and who's going to be observer at the next county supervisors' meeting. A little bit of music is played by the guitarists and five-string banjo players, and some poems come down from five or six people who are really good — speaking to what is happening *here*. They shine a little ray of myth on things; memory turning to legend.

It's also useful to raise a sum of money for a local need with a benefit poetry reading, and it's good to know this can be done successfully maybe twice a year. It works, a paying audience comes, because it's known that it will be a strong event. Sooner or later, if a poet keeps on living in one place, he is going to have to admit to everyone in town and on the backroads that he writes poetry. To then appear locally is to put your own work to the real test — the lady who delivers the mail might be there, and the head sawyer of the local mill. What a delight to mix all levels of poems together, and to see the pleasure in the eyes of the audience when a local tree, a local river or mountain, comes swirling forth as part of proto-epic or myth. (Michael McClure once said his two favorite provincial literary periodicals were *Kuksu,* "A Journal of Northern California Backcountry Writing," and *The New York Review of*

Books. Two poetry-reading invitations that I count as great honors were to the Library of Congress, and the North San Juan Fire Hall.) It is a commitment to place, and to your neighbors, that — with no loss of quality — accomplishes the decentralization of poetry. The decentralization of "culture" is as important to our long-range ecological and social health as the decentralization of agriculture, production, energy, and government.

By the "ethno-botanist" shoot from that sixties root I mean the roving specialists and thinkers in poetics, politics, anthropology, and biology who are pursuing the study of what it would mean to be citizens of natural nations; to be part of stable communities; participants in a sane society. We do this with the point in mind that the goal of structural political change is not a crazy society, but a sane one. These are in a sense studies in post-revolutionary possibilities, and in the possibilities of making small gains now; "forming the new society within the shell of the old." Such are (and though I list them here it doesn't mean they necessarily agree with all or anything I say) Bob Callahan and associates at Turtle Island foundation; Peter Berg and the Planet Drum group; Joe Meeker, Vine Deloria, Jr., and others working on the "new natural philosophy"; The Farallones Institute; Jerome Rothenberg and the *New Wilderness Newsletter;* Dennis Tedlock and *Alcheringa* magazine; Stewart Brand's *Co-Evolution Quarterly;* the long list of useful publications from Richard Grossinger and Lindy Hough; the Lindisfarne Association; New Alchemy; and in another more technical dimension, Stanley Diamond's work and his journal *Dialectical Anthropology. Organic Gardening* and other Rodale Press publications, with their consistent emphasis on *health* as the basic measure, might also belong on this list. There are others; I'm not even mentioning poetry magazines in this context. As a sort of ethno-botanist myself, I make the following offering:

IV

Poetry as song is there from birth to death. There are songs to ease birth, good luck songs to untie knots to get babies born better; there are lullabies that you sing to put the babies to sleep — Lilith Abye — ("get away Negative mother image!"); there are songs that children sing on the playground that are beginning poetries —

> baby baby suck your toe
> all the way to Mexico

> Kindergarten baby
> wash your face in gravy

> (I get these from my kids) or

> Going down the highway, 1954,
> Batman let a big one, blew me out the door —
> wheels wouldn't take it,
> engine fell apart,
> all because of Batman's supersonic fart.

(If you start poetry teaching on the grade school level, use rhyme, they love it. Go with the flow, don't go against it. Children love word play, music of language; it really sobered me up to realize that not only is rhyme going to be with us but it's a good thing.) And as we get older, about 11 or 12 years, we go into the work force and start picking strawberries or drying apples; and work songs come out of that. Individually consciously created poetry begins when you start making up love songs to a sweetie, which are called courting songs. Then, some individuals are sent out in adolescence to see if they can get a power vision song all by themselves. They go out and come back with a song which is their own, which gives them a name, and power; some begin to feel like a "singer." There are those who use songs for hunting, and those who use a song for keeping themselves awake at night when they are riding around slow in circles taking care of the cows. People who use songs when they haul up the nets on the beach. And when we get together we have drinking songs and all kinds of communal pleasure gathering group music. There are war songs, and particular specialized powerful healing songs that are brought back by those individuals (shamans) who make a special point of going back into solitude for more songs: which will enable them to heal. There are also some who master and transmit the complex of songs

139

and chants that contain creation-myth lore and whatever ancient or cosmic gossip that a whole People sees itself through. In the occident we have such a line, starting with Homer and going through Virgil, Dante, Milton, Blake, Goethe, and Joyce. They were workers who took on the ambitious chore of trying to absorb all the myth/history lore of their times; and of their own past traditions, and put it into order as a new piece of writing and let it be a map or model of world and mind for everyone to steer by.

It's also clear that in all the households of non-literate ordinary farming and working people for the past fifty thousand years the context of poetry and literature has been around the fire at night — with the children and grandparents curled up together and somebody singing or telling. Poetry is thus an intimate part of the power and health of sane people. What then? What of the danger of becoming provincial, encapsulated, self-righteous, divisive — all those things that we can recognize as being sources of mischief and difficulty in the past?

That specialized variety of poetry which is the most sophisticated, and is the type which most modern poetry would aspire to be, is the "healing songs" type. This is the kind of healing that makes whole, heals by making whole, that kind of doctoring. The poet as healer is asserting several layers of larger realms of wholeness. The first larger realm in identity with the natural world, demonstrating that the social system, a little human enclave, does not stand by itself apart from the plants and the animals and winds and rains and rivers that surround it. Here the poet is a voice for the nonhuman, for the natural world, actually a vehicle for another voice, to send it into the human world, saying there is a larger sphere out there; that the humans are indeed children of, sons and daughters of, and eternally in relationship with, the earth. Human beings buffer themselves against seeing the natural world directly. Language, custom, ego and personal advantage strategies all work against clear seeing. So the first wholeness is wholeness with nature.

The poet as myth-handler-healer is also speaking as a voice for another place, the deep unconscious, and working toward integration of interior unknown realms of mind with present moment immediate self-interest consciousness. The outer world of nature and the inner world of the unconscious are brought to a single focus occasionally by the work of the dramatist-ritualist artist-poet. That's another layer. Great tales and myths can give one tiny isolated society the breadth of mind and heart to be *not* provincial and to know itself as a piece of the cosmos.

The next layer, when it works, is harder: that's the layer that asserts a level of humanity with other people outside your own group. It's harder actually because we are in clear economic dependence and interrelationship with our immediate environment; if you are gathering milkweed, fishing, picking berries, raising apples, and tending a garden it shouldn't be too difficult to realize that you have some relationship with nature. It's less obvious what do we do with the folks that live on the other side of the mountain range, speaking another language; they're beyond the pass, and you can faintly feel them as potential competitors. We must go beyond just feeling at one with nature, and feel at one with each other; with ourselves. That's where all natures intersect. Too much to ask for? Only specialists, mystics, either through training or good luck arrive at that. Yet it's the good luck of poetry that it sometimes presents us with the accomplished fact of a moment of true nature, of total thusness:

Peach blossoms are by nature pink
Pear blossoms are by nature white.

This level of healing is a kind of poetic work that is forever "just begun." When we bring together our awareness of the world-wide network of folktale and myth imagery that has been the "classical tradition" — the lore-bearer — of everyone for ten thousand and more years, and the new (but always there) knowledge of the worldwide interdependence of natural systems, we have the bio-poetic beginning of a new level of world poetry and myth. That's the beginning for this age, the age of knowing the planet as one eco-system, our own little watershed, a community of people and beings, a place to sing and meditate, a place to pick berries, a place to be picked in.

The communities of creatures in forests, ponds, oceans, or grasslands seem to tend toward a condition called climax, "virgin forest" — many species, old bones, lots of rotten leaves, complex energy pathways, woodpeckers living in snags and conies harvesting tiny piles of grass. This condition has considerable stability and holds much energy in its web — energy that in simpler systems (a field of weeds just after a bulldozer) is lost back into the sky or down the drain. All of evolution may have been as much shaped by this pull toward climax as it has by simple competition between individuals or species. If human beings have any place in this scheme it might well have to do with their most striking characteristic — a large brain, and language. And a consciousness of a peculiarly self-conscious order. Our human awareness and eager poking, probing, and studying is our beginning contribution to planet-system energy-conserving; another level of climax!

In a climax situation a high percentage of the energy is derived not from grazing off the annual production of biomass, but from recycling dead biomass, the duff on the forest floor, the trees that have fallen, the bodies of dead animals. Recycled. Detritus cycle energy is liberated by fungi and lots of insects. I would then suggest: as climax forest is to biome, and fungus is to the recycling of energy, so "Enlightened Mind" is to daily ego mind, and art to the recycling of neglected inner potential. When we deepen or enrich ourselves, looking within, understanding ourselves, we come closer to being like a climax system. Turning away from grazing on the "immediate biomass" of perception, sensation, and thrill; and reviewing memory, internalized perception, blocks of inner energies, dreams, the leaf-fall of day-to-day consciousness, liberates the energy of our own sense-detritus. Art is an assimilator of un-felt experience, perception, sensation, and memory for the whole society. When all that compost of feeling and thinking comes back to us then, it comes not as a flower, but — to complete the metaphor — as a mushroom: the fruiting body of the buried threads of mycelia that run widely through the soil, and are intricately married to the root-hairs of all the trees. "Fruiting" — at that point — is the completion of the work of the poet, and the point where the artist or mystic re-enters the cycle: gives what she or he has done as nourishment, and as spore or seed, to spread the "thought of enlightenment" and this practice of reaching into personal depths for nutrients hidden there, back to the community. The community and its poetry are not two. In finishing, this poem:

FOR ALL
Ah to be alive
    on a mid-September morn
    fording a stream
    barefoot, pants rolled up,
    holding boots, pack on,
    sunshine, ice in the shallows,
    northern rockies.

rustle and shimmer of icy creek waters
stones turn underfoot, small and hard as toes
    cold nose dripping
    singing inside
    creek music, heart music,
    smell of sun on gravel.

    I pledge allegiance.
I pledge allegiance to the soil
    of Turtle Island
and to the beings who thereon dwell
    one ecosystem
    in diversity
    under the sun
with joyful interpenetration for all.

#

Based on talks given at Brown and Oberlin, FAU 40078

NOTES ON AUTHORS

The long-time Alaskans represented in this book are GARY HOLTHAUS, poet and teacher who now serves as Executive Director of the Alaska Humanities Forum; JOHN HAINES, poet who trapped in interior wilderness for 24 years; WALTER PARKER, Anchorage land planner elected and appointed to numerous influential municipal and state government positions; MARGARET MURIE, who grew up in Fairbanks and shared extensive wilderness experiences with her naturalist husband; and JOSEPH MEEKER, whose young adult life in urban and rural communities provided him with insights into the character of Alaskans.

Other writers are Alaska watchers: THOMAS LEDUC, Oberlin historian of United States land policies; MONROE PRICE, UCLA law professor concerned about the effect of the Alaska Native Claims Settlement Act on the lives of Alaska Natives; ROBERT DURR, an English professor who took time out from academia to study results of a recent state-sponsored Open-to-Entry recreational land program; WILLIAM KLOEFKORN, Nebraska poet, hog-caller, English professor and discovered of Alaska only in 1979; and GARY SNYDER, poet and resident of the Sierras, with a compelling ecological orientation derived in part from his study of the American Indian.

Most of the essays in this book are adapted from conference or workshop lectures delivered in various communities of Alaska between 1973 and 1979 under the sponsorship of the Alaska Humanities Forum.

INDEX